When Life Gives You Lemons...Stop Making Lemonade

When Life Gives You Lemons...Stop Making Lemonade
Practical Solutions to Navigating Life's Sour Points
By Leesa Askew

Edition 2019

Published by Conviction 2 Change Publishing Co.
www.conviction2change.com

Library Congress Control Number: 2019915731
ISBN: 978-1-7327121-4-0

Cover Design: Kayla Nicole Rodriguez

Editors: Align Editorial, Taylor D. Duckett

When Life Gives You Lemons...Stop Making Lemonade

Practical Solutions to Navigating Life's Sour Points

Leesa Askew

Foreword by Rahman Johnson

Conviction 2 Change Publishing Co.
www.conviction2change.com

Table of Contents

Dedication

eath is sour. The permanence can take your breath away as you grieve the loss of the ones you love. Reflecting on their life and all the lessons you've acquired is timeless. Sharing the lessons with others keeps their wisdom alive and valuable to others. Facing grief in the face is a way to stop making lemonade.

This book is dedicated with gratitude to the legends in my family and close network that have transitioned from this Earth.

My Father Herman Washington, you preached accountability to me before I even knew what it really meant. Each day I grow and understand the value you created for me and how the principles you've instilled in me are evergreen.

My Paternal Grandparents Ephraim & Thelma Washington, all the stories and wisdom you shared with me during our walks and times just sitting and sharing have overflowed my spirit. Living with the two of you, along with my aunt, during my adolescent years helped shape my resilience.

My Maternal Grandmother No Tok Yi, your bravery from a humble mountain village in South Korea to make an everlasting impact in the United States is an inspiration. You showed me what it meant to be loved unconditionally.

My Uncle George Washington, you were the first person that explained to me that failures are the way to grow and learn. Your strength and encouragement through my grief from the loss of your brother laid a strong foundation for me to give that same support to others.

My Bonus Grandmother Willie Mae Thorpe your commitment to health and wellness by consuming nutritionally dense food and herbs elevates me to live my best life. Your entrepreneurial spirit engaged and fascinated me as a teenager and has added to my courageous solopreneur pursuit.

My Teacher/Bonus Dad Franklin Smith, your belief in me in a time when I doubted myself the most, changed the trajectory of my life. Your ability to extract the best from all people has helped me do the same to everyone I encounter.

My Childhood Babysitter Gerry Gleason, in my elementary years witnessing your dedication as a devoted wife & mother impacted me so deeply in my soul that it manifests in my motherhood journey.

Foreword by Rahman Johnson

My life's path has shown me that there are no good days or bad days. Each life experience carries with it a lesson, but the question is – *am I prepared to learn?* How do you get prepared to learn? You learn through your daily experiences.

Life's lessons can present themselves like lemons – bitter and sour. Though we may want to avoid eating them, tasting them helps prepare you for growth and transformation. It's tempting to want to make them sweet by turning them into lemonade. However, turning them into lemonade is a way to misunderstand the true lesson. I've experienced quite a few lemony lessons in my life. Some I diluted and made into lemonade while others I faced. The lemons that I have faced have made me into the man I am today.

Twenty plus years ago, I was a proud undergraduate at Edward Waters College. While juggling a full class schedule I worked full-time as a Production Assistant for the CBS affiliate in Jacksonville, FL. Balancing life's sour points was a necessity to keep my head above water. I remember my grandmother always reminding me to not just talk about change but to embody the change that I wanted to see in the world. I was ready to see change in my hometown. At 20 years old, instead of complaining, I decided to run for public office. I ran to represent Group 5 as a commissioner on the Duval Soil and Water Conservation District.

Running for office provided an opportunity to take supreme accountability by working in my community and encouraging other young people to get involved to promote change and growth in my community. Galvanizing a coalition of student government leaders from the four colleges in Jacksonville, we walked every precinct in the city. I witnessed discrimination firsthand based on my race, age, and perceived level of ability. Despite those lemons, and with minimal funds, my team and I earned more than 80,000 votes from the city of Jacksonville! It was unprecedented! We won and victory was bliss!

After the election, things went well for two years. Then, out of nowhere, one of the biggest lemons I have ever faced presented itself when a political opponent filed charges against me with the State Ethics Commission. I was falsely accused of improperly obtaining a city mobile phone, using city vehicles, and misusing my position. I was out done. It was as if everything I had worked for was unravelling at that moment. As I defended myself in both the media and to the commission, I received some of the best advice ever. It was a defining moment. One advisor simply said, "Shut up. Just stop trying to respond to everything. Now, focus. You're so worried about everything, but the only person who is condemning you right now is *you,* and that will not help *you* in the long run."

Those words were exactly what I needed to hear. I knew that I had done nothing wrong, so I immediately stopped putting energy into this bitter and piercing lemon. I refused to allow what people thought fuel my responses. I elevated my own process and I stood still. I focused on learning from the experience. Once I faced the lemon, before I knew it, there was an article on the front page of the local paper saying that the accusations were dismissed!

Several years later when my term ended, I ran for State Representative and lost. Though defeated, I spent less time focused on the fact that I had lost an election that I was favoured to win, and more time learning! I learned that the lesson was not about winning but it was in the running. It was in all the lives that I connected with. It was in all the stories that I heard. It was in the fact that even after losing the election, I was invited to sit on a committee to help change education funding in Florida, which was one of the main reasons that I ran!

There were so many valuable lessons that came out of these experiences. All those nuggets that I picked up, prepared me to sit on one of the biggest platforms on the planet – Nickelodeon. A year after I lost the election, I became the host of their flagship show! Each sour point provided lessons that made me stronger and prepared me for life's future challenges. That's what this book is about. It is about using the lemons that life provides in order to help yourself and those around you. Making lemonade is the temporary fix. It makes things seem good until the lemonade is gone but you're still left with lemons to deal with.

I've known Leesa Askew for nearly 30 years. In that time, she has shown grace, dignity, poise and the willingness to face the lemons in every situation of *her* life. Years ago, as journalism majors in college and aspiring TV Reporters and Anchors, Leesa and I were tapped to host a television show in our home city. We were together more than we were with our families. In fact, during that time Leesa became my family!

I don't ever remember a time when the cameras were rolling (or even if they weren't) that Leesa wasn't wearing a smile. It was if she knew back then the power of the law of attraction. She innately knew that to attract those things that she wanted, she had to tune her frequency to the right channel. Her energy was and is still infectious.

I was there when life handed Leesa one of her most tragic lemons, the passing of her father. She could not control that, but her response was powerful. She handled it as she handled everything in her life, with grace and class. She shared her strength with me when my mother made her transition. During that journey, she reminded me of my ability to make it through this and was always there with that signature smile.

Yes, my friend has had personal and public struggles, but she's handled them with dignity. That's why when Leesa tells you to "STOP MAKING LEMONADE" she's uniquely prepared to share and inspire all of us to take extreme ownership of our lives. As you read *When Life Gives You Lemons...Stop Making Lemonade,* you will feel that same trademark smile in her words. As you read, feel the energy of the possibilities that exist when you reject victimization and decide to face all your sour points, and turn them into opportunities for personal growth. Doing the work will help turn your lemons into an elixir of bliss and greatness!

Enjoy the journey as you begin to live your best life!

Rahman Johnson

Actor, Producer, Host, Marketing Consultant and Founder of the Rahman Experience
www.rahmanjohnson.com

Introduction

hen life gives you lemons...we are no
longer making lemonade! It's time to
stop watering down and oversimplifying
our problems. Instead, it's time to take
personal responsibility and get rid of
life's lemons, regardless of their origin. While the origins of
some lemons are unknown, others can be pinpointed to specific
behaviors and moments of action, or inaction. *When Life Gives
You Lemons...Stop Making Lemonade* is going to provide you
with practical solutions to identify and eradicate your unwanted
lemons.

I feel that my life is testament to old adage, *"when life
gives you lemons..."* I have always had an affinity for lemons,
but that doesn't mean that I constantly want them around. My
earliest experience with the lemon was on a hot summer day. It
must have been about 90 degrees outside, and my shirt was
sopping wet with sweat. My body was full of little kid energy and
I remember running into the house and asking my mother for
a cool, delicious drink. I saw the lemons on the cutting board
and before she could stop me, I had taken a sliver of the lemon
into my mouth.

My immediate reaction was to scrunch up my face and shout, *"Ew!" "This was so sour,"* I thought. *"How could anyone want to eat this?!"* My mother laughed and laughed. She then gave me a glass of lemonade, asking if I still wanted something to drink. I looked from the glass in my hand to the lemons on the board. I had no idea how a drink from that sour fruit could possibly be any good. My mother urged me to give the lemonade a chance and drink it. I sipped it down and it was such a tasty drink! It was tangy and rich, with a citrus undertone that was smoothed over with the sweetness of sugar. I wondered how I could have overlooked such a wonderful treat, and I couldn't believe that such a sour fruit could yield such goodness.

As I got older, I began to realize that though lemonade is in fact very tasty, like all good things, moderation was key. I also realized that just because it tasted good, didn't mean it was good for me. In one season, as I was continuing my tried and true practice of making lemonade, I began to realize that I was starting to have more lemons than I could possibly convert into lemonade. It was then that I stopped, and began to wonder, why am I still making lemonade out of the same lemons, and where are these lemons coming from?

When problem after problem began to arise, I began to get tired of hearing, *"when life gives you lemons...make lemonade."* I know that those who said it meant well and were only passing on the advice that they had been given. It's easy to want to make lemonade but, is that the most beneficial way to problem solve? When you continually make lemonade, all you do is hide the problem under sugary sweet pretenses, but you never actually get to the root of it. When life hands you lemons, perhaps life is handing you an opportunity to make a change, but perhaps not the change you think, or the one that is most popular.

You may be thinking, "is it ever acceptable to make lemonade?" The answer is: sometimes. When life hands you situations that are beyond your control such as the loss of a family member, being laid off, having a life changing accident, getting to the root may not be the most productive use of your time and energy. When dealing with uncontrollable life events, asking "why" may only lead you into unhealthy places that transform your lemon into a lime. In those instances, as you seek to grapple with the presence of unknown, and unwanted variables, you'll need to find joy in the midst of what life is carrying you through. You'll need to find a way to sweeten up the situation that you're not sure how to stomach; lemonade may be the solution.

Though the situations mentioned above are major life lemons that should not be overlooked or ignored, they are not the primary focus of this book. *When Life Gives You Lemons...Stop Making Lemonade* focuses on those lemons that are within our control as we work to take ownership over the areas of our life that are out of alignment or unproductive. When you are handed lemons, be grateful. You have been gifted the moment to be introspective and self-reflective. It's an opportunity to change direction, and to do something wildly different.

When the next bitter lemon appears in your life, resist the urge to make something tolerable. Take a moment to explore the lifeline of the lemon. Life's lemons are about opening your eyes to the vast array of options around you.

Reflecting on what led you to that sour moment, and how you can change the tide, is when true transformation occurs. Ask yourself the Five W questions: what, when, who, where, and why, to cover the basics and help you understand the situation and context to pinpoint the origin of your lemon harvest. We are creatures of habit, and this evaluation process will help you step out of your comfort zone. This is your first step toward the best version of yourself. This step will cause your brain to rewire itself, which is uncomfortable, but growth and change are birthed from uncomfortable moments.

If you enjoy your life of endless lemonade, you may not be ready for this book. However, if you are tired of gulping down gallons of lemonade that provide no return on investment, this book is perfect for you. Much like the way lemons enter our lives, this book does not have to be read in a sequential manner. Pinpoint the lemons that are your biggest sour issues and indulge in those chapters first. There is also a Lemon Ledger with all the solutions available to you in one convenient section. The sweetest solution to a problem is its resolution.

As you read through this book, let's create a community of accountability. Please share one of your lemons with me on Facebook, Twitter, Instagram, or LinkedIn. Create your post with the hashtag, #stopmakinglemonade. Let's support one another. Join me in the movement to take supreme accountability to change the narrative and STOP making lemonade.

Chapter 1

Know Thy Lemons, Know Thy Self

> **Lemon Drop:** *The earliest account of lemonade was discovered in Egypt, around AD 1000. It was also a favorite with the famous Mongol emperor Wu Lai during the turn of the 14th century, who called the lemony concoction, "Lemon Hot Water," and even made a tune about it. King George the III of England much preferred lemonade over wine. This drink shared a big moment of fame when pop star Beyoncé named an album after this refreshing drink. Lemonade has evolved to include raspberries, strawberries or any number of fruits, as well as alcohol and other carbonation on occasion. For a sweet lemon treat, turn to page 7.*

L emons are defined by Merriam Webster as: 1) an acidic fruit that is botanically a many-seeded pale yellow oblong berry produced by a small thorny citrus tree and that has a rind from which an aromatic oil is extracted and 2) Something that is unsatisfactory or defective. As we can see from the definitions, lemons aren't like other fruits. They aren't shiny and pretty and they aren't afraid to grow on the tree exactly as they are, a warning to predators who may try to eat off the tree and discover that the fruit isn't as sweet as one might think.

Both definitions of lemons are applicable to our day-to-day lives. We are all aware that lemons can be converted into lemonade, but we need to move beyond that. It is important to be able to see past the potential allure of the lemon to identify the source of its sourness. We may have also experienced times in our lives where we were sold, or voluntarily picked, a lemon. Imagine how you felt in that moment, probably upset. When beginning the process of unearthing the hidden root causes of various issues, we must be able to identify those structures, or lemons, in our life that are poorly made and therefore defective. However, before we can do either of those things, we must be willing to name and call out our lemons.

Naming Your Lemons

The act of naming is an extension of power because words carry weight; they matter. That's why the old saying, "sticks and stones may break my bones, but words will never hurt me," is not entirely true. When you name a problem, you are calling it out, thereby decreasing its power. The lemons that you do not name are the lemons that become increasingly sour with time. They may become so sour that eventually, no amount of sugar can cover it up. When you don't address your lemons by name, you create a façade which is difficult, if not impossible, to maintain. The list of potential lemons is endless, but some of the lemons that we will address and work through in this book are the following:

⟢   Introspective Lemons

- ⬲ Relationship Lemons
- ⬲ Professional Lemons
- ⬲ Financial Lemons

Of course, this is not an exhaustive list, and new lemons can appear regularly. Also, as expressed in the introduction, you can't account for every possible lemon life may present you. However, the practical solutions you will be exposed to can be adjusted and applied as needed. If you have lemons that are in categories that weren't listed above, feel free to jot them down and call them out in the Noteworthy Lemons section.

Controlling the Degree of Sourness

"All that you touch, you change. All you change, changes you. The only lasting truth is Change." – Octavia E. Butler, Parable of the Sower

People tend to be resistant to change. It's human nature to desire to control everything. That's not possible. We're fond of the idea that if we think hard enough, the universe will bend to our will; and yes, to some extent, it may be true. How we think can often influence our actions, our perspectives, and how we respond to things in our lives. However, not everything is within our control. We live in a universe that is random. Our galaxy is rife with atoms and molecules that drift, shift, and change on a whim. Life can be the same way. You can plan for all the contingencies, and suddenly, something happens that will change things.

Life is not about trying to order a dynamic universe. It is instead often about adaptability. It is about the potential for change and the willingness to do so. Things can turn on a dime, and if you're not ready and willing to go with the flow and accept that not everything can be accounted for, you'll find yourself deeply disappointed. Instead of disappointment, think of your lemon. Think of your opportunity to do the best thing in spite of the circumstances.

The sooner we relinquish the need to control everything, to achieve the illusion of perfection, the sooner life will fall into balance. Though change is inevitable, we are able to control how sour our lemons become. This "control" is moreso an ability to tailor a response that is suitable to the problem(s) at hand. Every day we make decisions and are able to decide for ourselves what our response(s) will be. When lemon after lemon presents itself, it's easy to want to panic, or go into hiding (make lemonade), but you have to ask yourself, is that really the most efficient way to address the situation? Furthermore, if you respond poorly, are you really addressing the situation, or are you merely making matters worse? Charles Swindoll provides some insight on attitude and the energy that you are sending out into the world.

> *The longer I live, the more I realize the impact of attitude on life. Attitude, to me is more important than facts. It's more important than the past, than education, than money, than circumstances, than failures, than successes, than what other people think of or say or do. It is more important than appearances, giftedness, or skill. It will make or break a company, a church, a*

home. The remarkable thing is we have a choice every day regarding the attitude we will embrace for the day. We cannot change our past. We cannot change the fact that people will act in a certain way. We cannot change the inevitable. The only thing we can do is play on the one string we have, and that is attitude. I am convinced that life is 10% what happens to me and 90% how I react to it. And so, it is with you – we are in charge of our attitudes.

Weighing an average of 49 ounces, our brains are the source of how we perceive situations. Having an outlook and attitude of searching for the best will provide you with the power to construct your own narrative. We can't change the number of pages in our book of life, but we can change what is written.

In India, there is a religious figure named Kali. Kali is known as "The Destroyer." Kali is what happens when things break down or become obsolete. She is considered the purveyor of "things that happen outside your control." You would think that her image as deity would be one that is vilified, and that she would be looked upon with fear. However, she is considered a mother, a nurturer. If you're confused, think about this: she is considered so because even as things are destroyed or laid to waste, it lays the groundwork for a beginning. This deity is highly celebrated for the beginning of things in life and renewal. Many of her worshippers believe that there can't be anything new without getting rid of the old. And in truth, that's how life works. Life teaches us ways to adapt, change, and grow. Think about that the next time the universe gives you a lemon.

You can't change that you've got it. You have it in your hands. Now think. What will you do with it?

Am I Over Sweetening?

Have you ever had an experience in which, you are tasting someone's food and it's extremely over seasoned? You play along as to not offend, but secretly you are wondering how much more you'll be able to stomach. Sometimes the over seasoning is unintentional, however, it can also symbolize trying to cover up a lackluster dish. When it comes to addressing your lemons, you have to ask if you are adding too much to the lemon, or lemonade, and making it something that it's not. All lemons can be considered problems, but not all problems are lemons. We need to keep things in perspective so that you are not spending valuable time and energy excavating and uprooting things that you are meant to walk through. Your most painful experiences can yield the most power.

Changing your mentality from lemonade to a solution-based approach will take time. Your picking up this book shows that you're ready to, or at least considering, change your life and own up to your role in its current state. If you're not ready to tackle life's sour moments head on, enjoy a sweet treat, one final cup of lemonade.

Sweet Lemon Treat: *Traditional Homemade Lemonade*

Ingredients:
- 6 to 8 lemons
- 6 cups of cold water
- 1 cup of white sugar

Preparation: Wash the lemons thoroughly with warm water or vegetable cleaning spray. Roll the lemons between your hands and a cutting board to release the oils and juices. Slice the lemons into halves. Juice the lemons either by hand or using a juicer. Use a strainer to remove the seeds. Combine the juice with water and add sugar. Stir. Adjust as needed. Serve over ice.

Lemon Lessons:

- For some of life's situations, making lemonade may not be appropriate; you have to get to the root, take supreme accountability, and stop the lemon at its source.

- Naming your lemons empowers you to call them out and identify them. The things you expose and address lose their power.

- How you react to the lemon determines the degree of its sourness. If you want less bitterness, manage your responses.

- As the saying goes, "Don't make a mountain out of a molehill." Make sure that you aren't over sweetening the situation, making it into something that it's not.

Lemon Checkpoint:

- 🍋 What are the most common lemons present in your life?

- 🍋 What are some strategies that you've used to handle life's sour moments?

- 🍋 Do you take ownership for your role in the problems that arise in your life? If you aren't, take a moment to reflect on why you aren't owning your reactions.

_____

_____

_____

_____

_____

_____

_____

_____

_____

_____

_____

_____

_____

_____

When Life Gives You Lemons...Stop Making Lemonade

_____

_____

_____

_____

_____

_____

_____

_____

_____

_____

_____

_____

_____

_____

_____

_____

_____

_____

_____

_____

_____

_____

Chapter 2

Introspective Lemons

> **Lemon Drop:** *There are many different varieties of lemons. The Citron Lemon for example is usually found in India near the border of Burma. It grows near the Himalayas and can be extremely heavy. Some of these fruits can grow to be 8 to 10 pounds! They aren't typically used for their juice. Instead, they are usually used for the oils found in their rind. The oils are especially useful for fragrances. The rind can be peeled and candied for a quick snack. In ancient times, people used the Citron for many different physical maladies, including stomach issues and as an antibiotic. When the juice was used in ancient times, it was often mixed with honey and used as an antidote for poisons. For a Sweet Lemon Treat, turn to page 33.*

The heaviest lemons are often those that we inflict on ourselves. We are all imperfect, and our actions, or inaction, reflect this. Society teaches us that we are supposed to eschew transparency and accountability. We live with a "the buck doesn't stop with me" mentality where no one wants to take responsibility. Instead, many want to point the finger at others for why their lives aren't the way they envisioned it. Remember, when you point the finger at someone else, there are always four that point back at you. Before looking at external lemons, you have to deal with what is often the biggest, and most challenging lemon of all – yourself.

Childhood and Adolescent Lemons

S ometimes, the root of your lemony problems requires you to go back a few years (or decades) to your childhood. Childhood and adolescence are referred to as your formative years for a reason. Often, what happens during these crucial years can shape your life for years to come.

Growing up, were you allowed free rein and never told no? Did you grow up in a household that was full of joy, laughter, and love? Were your parents those that believed that children should be seen and not heard? Were they controlling and overbearing? Did you have parents that were emotionally distant, and didn't provide you with the nurturing you needed? What was your socioeconomic status? Did you get bullied often? Were you the bully?

There are endless questions about your childhood that could be interrogated. The point is, you need to be willing to take a deep look into what you were exposed to that may have resulted in unwanted lemons. It doesn't matter how long ago your childhood may have been, whatever you don't address will fester. If you are trying to build, you always want to make sure that you have a solid foundation. If you don't, everything you build will eventually fall apart. Take time to fix the cracks in your foundation to ensure that you are building on solid ground.

One of my favorite roles in life is being Andersen's mom! He is an extremely bright and engaging seven-year-old. Sometimes, his inquisitiveness can test my patience, especially around the topic of food! Often, when I try to get him to eat something, he'll question me and ask why. I'm convinced that why is his favorite word. When I responded to him, "because I said so," my son's response took me by surprise. He was confident enough to let me know that he didn't appreciate the response, "because I said so," because it did not actually answer his question or satisfy his desire to learn. It was at that moment that I realized, telling children to comply simply because they are told to may be setting them up for a life of lemonade making.

I realized that each time I shut down my son's curiosity, his mind began to close off a bit which means that he was missing opportunities to develop his critical thinking and problem-solving skills. It's the problem-solving skills we neglect to refine throughout childhood and adolescence that give us a lemon crop we don't want in adulthood. When we take the time to ask why and are used to doing it from an early age, we are in a better place to stop making lemonade and begin solving our problems another way. Unfortunately, we can't protect our children from lemons their entire life, but we can give them the tools early on to eradicate and manage the seeds.

People Pleasing and The Chameleon Effect

Have you ever met someone who is so inconsistent that you have no idea who they really are? These people behave like chameleons. While it is good to be adaptable, there is a fine line between adaptability and being a flake. People choose to change their personas for a variety of reasons, such as needing to code switch at work, or as a means of protection. As stated earlier, there is nothing wrong with being flexible, but you have to understand your "why." Why is it that you are changing, and are you losing yourself in the process?

I lived a veiled life for a season, several seasons actually, until I got sick of it. I was always a person that was afraid to say "no." There were times in my career when I'd take on impossible projects, afraid of saying "no." I would take unfair criticism because I had been afraid of being seen as angry and combative. I'd taken on things I knew I was overqualified for, and not part of my job responsibilities, because I wanted to go along to get along. *Yes, I'll do that project for you even though this was your responsibility. Yes, I'll stay late and save this deal in spite of that fact I'll get no credit and will be passed over for that promotion...yet again. Yes, I'll plan this party, even though I have a million other obligations. Yes, I'll do that for you even though, you'd never do it for me. Yes, yes, yes!*

Saying "no," and filtering out what I didn't want wasn't a pretty process. It was painful, and it went against years of conditioning that said I had to be agreeable to everyone and everything. I didn't like to disappoint people; I didn't like feeling as if I was the reason someone's day wasn't going well. In the midst of all of this, I did some self-reflection and asked myself "why." I took a close look at the people I was saying "yes" too in the various areas of my life. Why did I want to be associated with people who did not value my authentic self? Did they contribute to my life in meaningful ways? Did they make me feel good about the things I did? Were they honest in constructive ways about what they thought? Did they give freely of themselves without asking anything in return? I realized that many of these people weren't those that should remain in my circle. They'd asked for time and resources with no thought to the costs, both real and emotional, to me. I'd gone out of my way for a few of them and had gotten very little in return. I had to wonder if perhaps I was better off without them in my life. Turns out—I was.

By allowing the toxic people to walk out of my life, I could focus on myself in ways that represented who I really was and who I could be. I didn't mourn the relationships, but what I thought the relationships were. I was in love with the potentiality of many things in my life. By seeing things as they were and finding who I was, I was able to figure out what I really wanted. I had to be honest with myself, which is never, ever easy. Things I'd always taken for granted that I thought were essential parts of myself were stripped away. Things I'd thought I liked because *everyone* likes those things I had to discard. I had to be okay with being alone and with my own thoughts. I had to be okay with being myself.

When you find yourself changing for other people, doing things just because it's expected or wondering if you're really happy, it's time to take a close look at those lemons. Life isn't handing you a moment of sadness, loss, or regret—instead, life is offering you the chance to be the best and most authentic version of yourself, which is always great. You can't find happiness and fulfillment without knowing who you really are. You can't begin a journey if you don't know where you're trying to go. It's not a one and done process either. You may have to constantly check and see if you're doing what's best for you. Are you going to that college because it is what you want or are you following your friends, a romantic partner perhaps? Are you taking that job because it's aligned with your passion and purpose? Or is it out of obligation and what others expect of you? Are you dating someone because it is a great match on paper even though in your heart, you know you love someone else?

Whatever it may be—choose your why, so that you are not living life as a chameleon with no one truly getting to know the real you. Once you identify your why, you will have found your lemon. What you choose to do with the lemon in that moment is up to you. I know that personally, I decided that discarding the many masks I was juggling was the best move for me. I was tired of being a chameleon. Plus, juggling multiple personas is tiring, and I greatly value my rest!

At times, you may need to make changes to your expression of self because you may be placed in an environment that stops you from embarking on that journey. For example, you may be a city girl or guy living in the country. Though you may have been able to convince yourself that you enjoy the slower pace, in reality, you miss and need what city life has to offer you. Conversely, if you're a person who prefers small towns, maybe the city isn't the best place for you, even if those around you think it is. There are those of us who are living in large homes that, while beautiful, are a financial drain. Yet, we stay in those situations in order to "keep up with the Joneses" out of fear of public opinion, even when we know that we're in over our heads.

As stated in Chapter One, knowing yourself means knowing and understanding your lemons. Before uprooting this particular lemon, you should also consider asking yourself,

"What is this particular lemon trying to teach me?" In this case the question may also be, "Am I being true to myself or am I a people pleaser?" Other questions to consider asking yourself in the presence of your lemon are as follows:

1. What is the worst that could happen if you did what you wanted versus what others expect of you?

2. Would the outcome of Question 1 really be that bad? Your answer to Question 2 will really help you decide which way is forward and how to move toward your goals, away from the land of false and unreasonable expectations.

Take a moment to reevaluate what you want to do with your life. It is your life after all; no one can live it but you. Sure, people can have an opinion but ultimately, it's all about who *you* see yourself as and what is comfortable for *you*. *You* have to live in that house, work that job, drive that car, and wear those clothes. You have to be completely comfortable with your life choices, inside and out.

If you come to find that you don't like the real you, it's time to do some introspection and be open to make the big changes. It won't be pretty, nor will it be instantaneous, but it will be worth it in the long run. So, when life's lemon fell down into my hands, I embraced it with earnestness, and I was able to ask my why. Why was I not being true to myself? Why was afraid? What could I do to be more in line with my thoughts, emotions and dreams? Once I decided to be this version of myself, I was not only happier and healthier, but I was a better person.

Lemon Solution #1: Evaluate the areas of your life where you often find yourself saying "yes," especially those circumstances where saying "yes" has not been in your best interest. Once identified, determine if those people, or things, are adding value to your life, or if they are an energy and resource drain.

It's Permissible, But Is it Profitable?

After reading these anecdotes about people pleasing and living as a chameleon, you may be seeing yourself and going, "me too." Freedom is a beautiful thing, but before you begin blasting Diana Ross's, "I'm Coming Out," pause and think for a moment. In *The Bluest Eye*, the late Toni Morrison introduced readers to the concept of being "dangerously free." Just because you can, doesn't mean that you should.

In this context, being true to yourself doesn't mean that you disregard others and don't take constructive criticism or feedback. That's not being true to yourself; that's being resistant to change, communication, and compromise. Being true to yourself involves understanding the things that make you tick and aligning those things with a value system that encourages honesty, fairness, and goodness to not only yourself, but others as well. It means that you don't stick to how others try to define you and instead seek to define yourself.

This is an important distinction because having self-respect and being true to yourself does not give you license to be rude, disrespectful, or outright hostile toward others around you. It simply means that you should be willing to be open and to be straightforward with others about your real expectations instead of hiding behind pretenses. People deserve to know the real you, and you deserve to be loved and respected for who you really are.

Lemon Solution #2: If you feel that the chameleon analogy applies to you, write down those aspects of your personality that have remained hidden, along with why and for approximately how long. Then, see if adjusting towards reclaiming those areas of your life can be made in a way that doesn't change you from a people pleaser into a jerk.

Victim Playing

I would like you to take a moment and think about those in your community. They can be family, friends, colleagues, or peers. Of all these people, can you identify the one person who constantly is playing the victim? Is that person you?

It's tempting to play the victim because doing so allows you to escape accountability and taking ownership. To be clear, there are instances when you or someone close to you is being victimized. In those cases, the person being victimized should be taken seriously and given the help they need to rectify the situation. Additionally, those who engage in victim playing as adults, were often victimized as children or adolescents. Self-victimization is a learned, adapted, behavior that serves as a coping method; it is the turning lemons not just into lemonade, but into a lemonade franchise, in order to avoid dealing with the underlying trauma.

When you repeatedly play the victim, you make yourself seem unstable and as though your word is unreliable. This can result in you missing out on opportunities and alienating those closest to you. Additionally, playing the victim creates unnecessary lemons in your life. Though you cannot change the past, and the pain that may have occurred, you do have a choice regarding what your future looks like. When you entertain those around you who play the victim, you are accepting lemons from others. Part of living lemon free and taking ownership is not taking on the lemons of others, no matter how tantalizing they may seem or how emotionally invested you are.

You may be playing the victim and aren't aware of it. It is also possible that you are fully aware of it but are unsure of how to change it. Before getting into how to tell if you, or those around you, are playing the victim, let's look at some of the "perks" of self-victimization.

- You begin to sound more interesting to others because you get to share stories of your past traumas. You hold on to these traumatic experiences like trophies.
- You are more likely to get what you want.
- Other people feel sorry for you and shower you with attention.
- You can manipulate your way out of uncomfortable situations, holding up your past traumas as a shield against critique.
- You don't have to take responsibility (ownership) for anything.

Now that you are aware of the "perks," here are indicators that this type of self-serving behavior is being exhibited by you, or those closest to you.

- You think that everyone is out to get you and perceive everything that doesn't go your way as a deliberate slight.
- You tend to be cynical, jaded, and pessimistic.

- You over sweeten your problems, blowing them out of proportion.
- You continually reopen past wounds to continue feeling like a victim.
- You complain, even when things in your life are going well.
- Constructive feedback is taken as a personal attack.
- You engage in negative self-talk.
- You keep company with those who also self-victimize and try to play "oppression Olympics."

In the reflection section, if you recognize any of these traits in yourself or those you love, jot them down along with ideas on how to counteract these lemon-producing behaviors.

Lemon Solution #3: Counseling is stigmatized within society because many take it as an implication that you are "crazy" or "unstable." However, to get to the root of self-victimization, help from a licensed professional may be appropriate and most effective. In the meantime, begin to make a timeline of your trauma, to see if the incidents intersect, or if they stem from distinctly different, roots.

Poor Time Management

Not all lemons result from extreme circumstances. One of the most common lemons is poor time management. This lemon, if not dealt with, can impact every area of your life and bring unnecessary stress. One manifestation of poor time management is procrastination. Procrastination never ends well because you end up delivering a rushed product instead of the high-quality work that you may be capable of. It is also based in fear, so the next time you find yourself procrastinating, perhaps you should ask yourself what you're afraid of or trying to avoid.

Another form of poor time management is when you aim to people please. When you overcommit yourself, you end up mismanaging your time. *No* is a declarative statement that requires no qualifications or explanations. Time is finite; to reduce these stressful lemons, protect yours at all cost. One way to help with this is to get organized. When we are organized, our day can start off without a lot of rushing around, and we can take a breather here and there if we know exactly where everything is. Getting organized at your home, office, and in your life helps to keep you focused on your goals. It also declutters your space and your mind so you can really see the big picture. Try scheduling a time throughout the month to declutter and spruce up your car, home, and desk. It will make you feel loads better and keep you on track.

Lemon Solution #4: Find out what you are afraid of that results in you procrastinating. Also understand that it is okay to be selfish with protecting your time. Block off your calendar or do what is necessary to ensure that you are not trying to fit more into each day than it can hold.

Lack of Self-Care

S elf-care has been in the news a lot lately as experts are encouraging more meditation and mindfulness. These concepts sound good, but they are only trendy buzz words if not properly actioned into a meaningful routine. Self-care doesn't need to be elaborate. You don't have to check yourself into some fancy retreat to achieve the goals and benefits of self-care. All you have to do is find a contemplative practice that brings you joy and helps keep you centered.

For many, your daily routine looks something like this: You wake up at 5 a.m. and jump out of bed. You may be exhausted from the night before, but you can't go back to sleep. You've got things to do. You may take a hasty shower and get dressed. You may even wake up your partner because you notice they're sleeping through their alarm. You may spend an hour or more in rush hour traffic as you try to maneuver as best you can around huge trucks and slow drivers, hoping to make the morning meeting. However, you know that you're probably going to be late.

Your boss is on you to do even *more* work than you already are, and by lunch time you want to scream. But you can't take a walk like you've been planning. Instead you say yes to things you probably shouldn't and work through lunch with only a salad. You're starving, but you're too busy to stop. You then have to rush out of work to deal with your family, and you still haven't made time to take a break. It's late at night, and you're still up late going over reports for the next day at work, and you know when you go to sleep, you're starting things all over again.

If this routine sounds familiar, you're not alone. We are often told that if we're not busy, we're not doing enough. We're constantly told that if we aren't feeling as if we're breathless and harried, we're not being productive enough. This has resulted in a society that's secretly suffering, secretly being burdened under the weight of *so many things to do*. We've been told that we have to cope, and we can't do any less and we can't say no, so we've been lulled into believing that taking time off for ourselves is tantamount to a sin. We're afraid to take our vacation days because we may be replaced by the next worker while we're gone. But if you make yourself sick while you're working or experience something life threatening, what will your company do anyway? They will replace you. But you can't replace yourself. You can't spell WIN if there is not an "I" which is why you must practice self-care.

Self-care is important for everyone. It's not something that should be taken lightly or brushed aside. We take our time to give our car a good tune-up, we fix our washing machines if they start making funny noises, and we bring in repairmen if our lights flicker or we notice a leak. You should treat your body the same way. Don't wait until a medical emergency forces you to take time to care for yourself. Do it before it gets to a critical juncture.

Self-care also isn't about being selfish. It's about knowing your limitations and respecting them. It's about understanding that you're not superhuman. It's about valuing your time and energy. Self-care is about doing what you can to preserve your emotional, physical, and psychological reserves. It's not being selfish. After all, you can't take care of anyone if you can't take care of yourself.

It's okay if you spend time taking care of yourself. It's okay if you take time to take stock of your health and your levels of energy. Taking care of yourself helps you to help others and keeps your lemon level down. It's the most valuable thing you can do for your family and those closest to you. See below for some examples of self-care.

Lemon Solutions #'s 5 – 13:

Eat Right – Stop eating on the run. Eating on the go exposes you to foods that are devoid of true nutritional value. Take some time to have a good, decent meal that's chock full of things you need like vitamins, minerals, and antioxidants. Eating right ensures that your body will be able to maintain your heart, lungs, and most importantly your brain (mind). Ensure you get the recommended daily amount of vegetables, fruits, and grains.

Drink Water – Hydrate yourself. We're 98% water and need H2O to power our skin, our hair, and our organs. Instead of settling for a soda, coffee, or juice, take things to a more basic level and drink water. If you want to drink water with a bang, try it with a bit of lemon.

Visit the Doctor – Regular check-ups are crucial to understanding the ways your body may be changing and growing. It's important to develop a relationship with a trusted medical professional and get regular screenings for your heart, eyes, lungs and any other potential issues. Cancer screenings are essential as we age, and for anyone who is sexually active, it's a must to have regular sexual wellness screenings. Make sure that you are doing all you can to be informed and stay in good health.

If you are a woman over the age of thirty-five don't feel embarrassed to get a mammogram. Breast cancer is a silent killer, and millions of women have been saved by just getting checked. Men should get checked for prostate cancer as part of their routine exams as they progress into their thirties as well.

Exercise – Thirty minutes a day is a great start! Take a walk around the block. Go for a jog. Get into the groove with a dance class or just dance around your house. Get out and get some fresh air and go biking on a trail. Take a friend or a close relative with you to keep you motivated. If you hate exercise, try something fun like Zumba or yoga. You can even do some low-impact water aerobics. Do what you like, but get your body moving so that you can get your heart pumping. Exercise helps to lower blood pressure and decrease stress. If you're a busy mom, a busy dad, or just plain busy, you probably can use a lot of that.

Decompress – Take time to read a book, watch a tv show you enjoy, or just watch videos of cute cats on YouTube. Whatever makes you relaxed, DO IT. Take a break and enjoy your day. Take a bubble bath or have a glass of wine. Do what it takes to get you feeling calm and serene. By decompressing, you are deactivating your flight or fight system. This will help reduce stress hormones like adrenaline and cortisol.

Talk to Someone – If you're going through a hard time like depression or experiencing suicidal ideations, it is imperative that you talk to a mental health professional. Even if you're feeling just a little stressed or out of sorts, having someone to help you talk through your issues can make you feel better about yourself and your situation. Don't think that your mental health should take a back seat. We live in a society that tells us "What doesn't kill you makes you stronger." But that's not always true.

Sometimes it may not kill us or do noticeable damage, but life stressors can take their toll, nevertheless. There's nothing shameful about going to therapy or talking to someone if you feel as if your burden is too great. And if you need to unload on a trusted friend or family member who can give you the support you need, you should do that. Depression affects millions of Americans a year and can put you at risk for a variety of ailments, including heart attack and high blood pressure.

Take Up a Hobby - If you're the kind of person who puts everyone first and everything else on the backburner, it may be time for you to find something you like to do. Whether it's backpacking through the country, knitting, playing tennis or swimming, find something that is special and fun for you and just do it! Get out there and get your blood pumping with a hobby that is not only a great fun but is a great passion. Remember, a hobby is something that works for you. If you've been secretly wanting to try your hand at something but are afraid of what others may think or of your skill level, well, there's nothing like seizing the moment! Don't live your life with regrets. Instead, think of an activity that would be invaluable to your mind and spirit and ignites your curiosity.

Say No - It's okay to just say no. If you don't have time for that PTA meeting, say so. If you would rather not participate in hosting Thanksgiving *yet again*, say so. We often feel as if we have to say yes to things that bring us stress in order to make others feel comfortable. Well, if you don't feel comfortable, there's no way you can really do that for others.

Get Some Sleep – We're bombarded by the message that sleep is for losers. In fact, one famous celebrity recently harangued an audience by stating that "You cannot sleep eight hours a day! Rich people don't sleep eight hours a day!" This is advice that is very crippling to men and women that already have round-the-clock duties. The truth is, we NEED sleep. It is one of our most basic biological functions. It is nearly as important as breathing. In fact, during an experiment years ago, soldiers were deprived of sleep for up to a week. After a few days, many of them began to have intense hallucinations and the experiment was forced to end. Another experiment had researchers waking people up right before they hit REM sleep. Many of them suffered ill physical effects, and this proved that not only do we need sleep, we need *quality* sleep.

After participants were allowed a full, uninterrupted night's sleep, they not only felt better but when they did sleep, they entered longer periods of REM sleep. REM (rapid eye movement) is often synonymous with dreaming. During this time, you can often see the eyes shifting back and forth beneath the eyelid. Therefore, the times that we dream are probably important for our brains. Neuroscientists don't know everything about our brains, but they do know that sleep and dreaming are important to our day-to-day health.

Sleep deprivation is associated with higher blood pressure, increased risk of diabetes, memory loss, and other health problems. So, don't listen to the mantra that you've got to grind 24/7. You can be successful in life and get a good night's sleep. In fact, evidence suggest that the way to be successful is to be happy, healthy, and focused. You can't do that if you're so tired you can't really think.

Keeping up with the grind and hustle culture is neither sustainable nor practical. When you don't practice self-care, lemons tend to show up en masse, because you don't have the energy to be your best self. Not only that—because you are so burnt out, you aren't going to be thinking about getting to the source of the problem. Instead, you'll be more inclined just make a quick glass of lemonade and move on. You can either be burnt out by the lemons themselves or strive to live in a balanced state that allows you to take ownership. The choice is yours.

One indicator that you are stressed or dealing with a plethora of lemons is oily skin. Interestingly enough, lemons can actually be used as an astringent to help clear up the skin. Take a look at how on page 33.

Sweet Lemon Treat: *Homemade Astringent for Oily Skin*

Ingredients:
- 1 ¼ cup distilled water
- 1/4 cup apple cider vinegar (any brand will do)
- 1/4 cup witch hazel
- 10 drops lavender oil
- 10 drops tea tree oil
- A few drops of lemon oil or lemon juice
- An 18 to 20 - ounce glass jar or bottle

Preparation: Add the distilled water and witch hazel to a glass jar. Next, add the apple cider vinegar, the lavender, tea tree and lemon oils or juices. Place a lid on the bottle or jar and shake the jar to blend the ingredients well. Store the mixture in a cool, dark place.

How to Use Mixture: Wash your face as usual with cleanser. Rinse. Pat dry and wash again with the homemade astringent. Let sit for a few seconds and then rinse well. Pat skin dry and moisturize.

Lemon Lessons:

- Sometimes you are the major source of your lemons.

- People pleasing can leave others wondering who you really are, and you can lose your sense of self in the process.

- Self-Victimizing can stem from past wounds, but if and how you choose to move beyond the pain is up to you.

- Poor time management is rooted in fear and impacts your ability to identify and deal with the lemons that continuously appear.

- Self-care is a must! If you want to maintain a healthy life and have energy to deal with all that life throws at you, you need to be able to unplug and reset. Constant burnout wears on your objectivity. Do you have a great self-care routine? Share it with us by using the hashtag #Lemoncare

Lemon Checkpoint:

- 🍋 What are the underlying reasons that you engage in people pleasing? How long has it been going on?
- 🍋 Which self-victimizing traits did you identify in your life, or the life of someone close to you, and how are you going to address them?
- 🍋 Do you have a self-care practice? How are you going to develop one?

_____

_____

_____

_____

_____

_____

_____

_____

_____

_____

_____

_____

_____

When Life Gives You Lemons...Stop Making Lemonade

Chapter 3

Relationship Lemons

Lemon Drop: *Lemons are used in the South for a variety of things, and desserts are a favorite. One of the most popular include "Magic Lemon Cups." Magic Lemon Cups are a part and parcel of Southern cuisine, and are the supposed brainchild of Fanny Farmer, a baker that lived during the 19th century. Her recipe is also known as "Lemon Pudding," and is famed for its delicious taste. This dessert is as versatile as it is great to eat. There is a light, fluffy layer of sponge that is separated by a thick lemon-type pudding on the bottom. This dessert is typically served warm in cups, and you can leave them as is, or flip them over and your guests can see the delicious cake on bottom topped with the tangy lemon pudding on top. For a sweet lemon treat, turn to page 65.*

Lemon Drop: *Love wearing white but dread how it fades and becomes—well—not so white? Well, did you know that you can keep your whites sparkling white with the power of the lemon? It's true! The citric acid in lemons helps to cut the dirt and grime. It's been a tried and true secret of beautifully attired men and women for years. Don't take our word for it. Grab a lemon and try it for yourself! For tips on how to whiten your clothes with lemons, turn to page 67.*

Some of the most deeply rooted, and difficult to deal with lemons are those caused by those closest to you, your family and friends. This is why you will often find that when seeking out counseling, one of the first topics of conversation is the relationships in your life. Our friends, families, and romantic partners can be our biggest source of support and joy, but they can also test our gangster on a regular basis! We are going to talk about those less-than-stellar moments, and how to address them in a healthy, wholesome way.

Generational Lemons

What is the first thing that comes to mind when you think of the word inheritance? For many, their first thoughts turn to money, cars, property, and other material things. Others may think about inheritance in terms of physical features. However, there are other inheritances, also transferred through the DNA, that have a profound impact on who we are as individuals.

Trauma is one such inheritance. There have been studies conducted that have shown that trauma can change the DNA of those exposed to it and can be passed on to their children. There isn't a genetic mutation, but it is possible for a child to have health or behavioral issues related to trauma experienced as far back as several generations ago. This genetic response to trauma is often seen in those who have been exposed to violence, poverty, and other extreme situations.

When we contextualize this, not all the lemons that are presently expressing themselves in our life may be entirely our own. These generational lemons become our own when we welcome them in and refuse to break the cycle. There is a popular meme that circulates that touches on this subject. It says, "Generational curses run in my family...this is where they run out." I love that meme because it's so true. We have our own lemons to deal with, do we really want to lug around generational ones as well?

Take a moment to think about what runs in your family. Now take a moment to think about your kids, or the kids you hope to have. Do you want them dealing with those same issues? If the answer is no, now is when you begin the difficult, but fruitful work, of uprooting what's harmful. Another popular meme is, "We are our ancestors' wildest dreams." If you truly desire this to be true, and to be able to honor those who came before you, you have to be unburdened by their baggage, even though they may not have intended to pass it to you.

Lemon Solution #14: Take a moment of self-reflection and make note of any harmful patterns that you see in the lives of your family members as well as in your own life. Ask the elders in your community, if they are available, where they think the root came from. Having done that, develop an action plan to counter these generational lemons. While doing this, also be sure to make note of the good fruit that you, or family members, have borne so that it can continue for future generations.

Marriage Lemons

One of the biggest sour points in my life was the day I married someone I knew wasn't right for me. I felt horrible thinking that I'd made a mistake. Like a puzzle with worn out edges, I wanted and tried to make the pieces fit. Just like puzzles, each piece has its perfect match if placed correctly, and we just weren't a perfect interlocking match.

My first husband and I had different value systems, different perspectives, and many areas of our lives didn't mesh well. Just finishing undergrad, I wanted what I thought was the next step in life at the time: a marriage, a family, and a new home. I wanted to be on what I perceived as the right track to building a solid foundation. Despite not feeling like this was the perfect match to my puzzle of life, I suppressed my instincts to maintain the happy "perfect" life facade.

Out of my network of friends I was the one that was *always* in a relationship. Everyone expected me to marry and have multiple children. I didn't want to disappoint. I was like that frequently. A people pleaser; I was the chameleon described in Chapter 2. I knew I wasn't ready for marriage. I had things I wanted to accomplish in life and career. I forfeited my acceptance to law school to be in this marriage and build the perfect family. I ignored all the red flags and blinking yellow hazard signs, because I let the fear of my so-called "biological clock" get in the way. I knew that I didn't love this man enough to spend the rest of my life with him, so I lied to myself. I told myself that it would work. I convinced myself that being in a marriage didn't mean you had to be 100% in love. I mean Tina Turner said it best with "What's love got to do with it?" I found other compensating factors to make up for the lack of love. I justified being with him because he had graduated college, had a good job, and his family was amazing. They treated me so well that it pushed me further from my personal truths and into super people pleaser mode.

My ex and I argued for months on end about every little thing leading up to the wedding. We argued about the color scheme, how much to spend, who to invite, and where to have the ceremony. We had a large wedding party and a guest list that kept growing. Our wedding was more of a production than a declaration of love and commitment. As if that wasn't enough, I broke my foot two weeks before the date! I postponed the wedding because it just had to be *perfect,* I thought. Really though, I didn't want to be married. Not at that time and not to that person. We argued all the way up until we were at the altar, and ultimately it did not last. My parents got divorced, and I didn't want to be another statistic, but I must admit signing my divorce papers, while painful, was ultimately freeing.

If you're unhappy in your marriage, it's highly likely that those feelings will spill out into other areas of your life. Those close to you will be able to discern that something is amiss, and it could impact your ability to reach your goals. We always talk about being equally yoked. This is crucial for success. We match with people for a variety of reasons, but taking supreme accountability means recognizing when our marriage is out of alignment. Sometimes, the alignment can be restored through mediation and counseling. However, sometimes you have to uproot the marriage and divorce. I don't want to make light of divorce, because it is a major life-changing event, and it hurts, but the question is do you want to drink the same bitter lemonade for a lifetime, or give yourself the chance to find something sweeter? Though I appreciate the lessons my first marriage taught me, had I not known when to call it quits, I wouldn't be happily married to a wonderful man, and we wouldn't have our amazing son.

Lemon Solution #15: When your marriage is in trouble, it can negatively impact your ability to perform well in other areas of your life. If you see that your union is becoming undone, try seeking counseling if you're both open to it and committed to making things better. However, if you have both reached an impasse, be mature enough to understand that instead of laying blame, sometimes it's simply that you two don't mix well together, meaning that making lemonade would be impossible.

Pick Your Friends Wisely

Being an extroverted only child, I both craved and enjoyed having a lot of friends. My mother would get upset because as a child I would always give away my toys to gain friends. I felt like the nicer you are the more people will want to hang out and be your friend. Who you choose to surround yourself with is telling, because it shows others how you view yourself. Just wanting to preserve my relationships, my friendship circle and my self-image were not mirroring one another. I knew that I was a strong, wise, and assertive person. But amongst certain friends, I was a chameleon and yes-woman. I learned the danger of this in a very tangible way.

I was once friends with a young woman named Samantha. She and I had met during a networking event.

Samantha dazzled me with her savvy sense of fashion and her style. We clicked instantly, and our friendship seemed so natural. At least, I thought so at the time. Looking back, it was anything but, yet, we ended up being friends for over a decade.

During that time, I had no problem loaning her money, helping her out with transportation, buying her food, etc. Other friends of mine would notice that I was going out of my way for her when she wasn't doing the same in return. I would scoff and say "Oh no. She's going through a hard time. I'm just helping her." I'd run myself ragged taking her places and bending over backwards to make sure she was all-set. I mistakenly thought that if I could control the narrative, if I could have her say "You've helped me so much. So, I can't even think of not being your friend," she'd stay in my life.

I slowly began to see the truth when I hired her boyfriend to design my website. I was going into event planning and wanted a site that would be chic and inviting. I didn't know where to begin as I wasn't very good at coding and website design at the time. I was telling her about it, and she told me I should hire her boyfriend. I had never met him face-to-face, and I was a little wary. "Oh no," she told me, "He's fantastic!" I spoke with him briefly over the phone and it was settled. The price seemed fair too. He only wanted me to buy a plane ticket for him to go with my friend to visit family in Canada. I agreed happily and looked forward to seeing the work.

Over the next week or so, it became apparent that he wasn't very knowledgeable. I told my friend about my concerns and she told me it would be fine, just give him a chance. I told her okay and continued to wait. Meanwhile, I purchased the ticket for his flight. The ticket was nonrefundable. I checked over the next few weeks and noticed nothing much had been done to the site. In fact, the little that had been done seemed wrong and amateurish. It looked horrible. I didn't feel comfortable showing anyone what I had seen. I told myself it was a work in progress. Her boyfriend called me frantic a few days later saying that he needed me to buy him another ticket on another flight. I was at a loss for words. The flight he wanted was twice as much as I had paid before! Neither he nor my friend offered to compensate me for the nonrefundable ticket. Determined to keep my friendship, I purchased the other ticket. Samantha and her boyfriend went on their trip, and, with the help of another friend who did not charge me a dime, I began building the website myself. I found the experience to not be as difficult as I imagined, and with a little studying and research, I soon had a nice-looking site.

Upon Samantha's return I found out that she and her boyfriend had broken up. She seemed reluctant to tell me why. Then she finally admitted that he had smuggled drugs onto the plane. She claimed she didn't know, but something in her tone told me that wasn't true. When I pointed out that I could have gotten into a lot of trouble because of her boyfriend smuggling contraband onto a flight, she dismissed my concerns and pointed out other things he had done to irritate her.

I began to see that her behavior was self-centered. She went on to do other things that proved that she was only concerned about what she could gain from our friendship. After a while, I began to say no to her requests. It all came to a head one day during a busy time at my job. Samantha called me, and I had back-to-back meetings scheduled with clients. She wanted me to create some documents for her. I asked her why she couldn't do it herself and she replied, "I just don't know how. Can you do it?" I asked her what the documents were for and when she told me, I knew exactly what she could do. "It's so easy. There's a template online that I use. I don't have time to send you the link as I'm running out the door, but I can tell you the company and site. Just download it from there." She wasn't satisfied. "Why can't you just do it for me?! I need it right now!" she demanded. I politely told her I was going to be at a meeting and that it was impossible to do. She hung up on me. I didn't think anything of it, and I thought maybe she just needed some time to cool off.

She texted me some time later. She said that she didn't think our friendship was going in the right direction and that after talking to her therapist, she'd decided I was toxic because it seemed like I couldn't think of anyone else's needs but my own. I was floored. I tried to contact her but found I had been blocked from her phone. I had been blocked from every social media account she was on. I had been blocked from her life. Friends are the family you choose. I mourned, and it hurt, because of how highly I regard my friends. I noticed that where there should have been a dark hole where her presence would have been, there was light. My life flourished. I slowly realized that *she* was the toxic one. After going over every scenario with her in my mind, I found that there was nothing I had done to prompt her actions. This was how she was, and there was nothing I could have done about it.

My other friends were relieved to see I had seen the truth about her. I began to realize that many of them had never enjoyed spending any time with her. They'd all grumbled about her self-centered and entitled attitude. She had had several friendships that ended abruptly, and it was never her fault. I had been blinded by it because I just saw the best in her and always thought she had the best intensions. She is an opportunist and will only engage when she was benefiting. Personal equity didn't mean anything to her because she was only concerned by the here and now. Even after she had cut off our friendship, I had tried to think of ways I could have saved it. Ways I could have done something, anything to make her understand that I was trying my best to be a good friend. I soon discovered that there was probably nothing I could have done.

Though it's sometimes tempting to bail out your family and close friends, all you are doing is over sweetening, and causing yourself additional stress. Instead of solving their problems for them, the best way to stop making lemonade is to sit them down and empower them with the tools to help themselves. I didn't have a chance to do this with Samantha and based on her personality, she probably would have rejected what I had to say. That's okay, you are not assigned or designed to help everyone. However, do the most good where you can, and that starts with critical problem-solving and holding those around you accountable for their messes.

Lemon Solution #16: Understand that in relationships, sometimes things get beyond your control. You can't control everything, especially how other people perceive you. The version of you that someone else has created is not your job to manage. When you see that your "friends" are draining you, step away from the lemon juicer and move on; your time and emotional capital are much too valuable.

Cut The Toxicity

W e have all had the misfortune of coming into contact with toxic people. In various seasons, we may have been the toxic person. When dealing with toxic people, making lemonade isn't a wise move because you end up poisoning yourself, and anyone else you have drink it. Toxic people and situations need to be disposed of and labeled as **hazardous** so that others will be aware of their sour behavior. You may be wondering to yourself, "Do I have any toxic people in my circle, or even worse...am *I* the toxic person in my circle?" Here are some general traits to help you identify toxic people, relationships, and situations.

Manipulation: This is a very serious sign, though it's one we often miss because we may not even know it's happening. Manipulation is often very subtle and plays on our inherent need for approval and affirmation. Manipulators can make everything your fault, even if it clearly isn't. You may find yourself apologizing for something *they* did! For example, you may have a family member that guilts you into doing things you don't want to do. They may say things like "You may not think family is important, but it is." So, you find yourself hosting a dinner or taking on some other task because the implication is that if you don't, you must not think family is important. See what happened there? Just the implication of not caring is enough to cause you to overcompensate! You think to yourself, "That isn't true! I'll prove it." That's exactly what manipulators want you to do.

Lemon Solution #17: If you are dealing with a manipulative person, the best way to deal with this kind of behavior (if you have to at all) is to set firm boundaries and stick to them. Reframe their manipulative statements in a way that promotes your agency. The manipulator may try to further engage you in their machinations by guilting you for it. Don't fall for it. Stick to your guns, set clear boundaries, and understand that yes, they may be angry and disappointed, but they need to take ownership of those feelings — not you.

Gaslighting: This is an extension of manipulation, but it is so insidious that it can wreck your self-esteem and feelings of self-worth. It comes from an old movie where a man decides to drive his wife crazy. He does so by lighting the gas lamps and making her think she did it. Then he blows them out and makes her think they were never lit in the first place. After a while, she begins to slowly go insane, and begins to question her ability to perceive events.

Gaslighting is one of the main functions of a toxic relationship. It basically allows the person who does it to rewrite events. It's kind of an "alternative facts," kind of thing. However, in this case, the "alternative facts," isn't the truth. Not by a long shot. You may confront a toxic person with something you remember them saying, and they'll say, "I never said that! You must be remembering things wrong!" or you may clearly remember something they did, and they may twist things around and say, "No, YOU did that. I was simply doing x,y, and z and that's how it happened."

If you're not vigilant, you may find yourself questioning how you feel, how you think, and how you remember things.

You may think to yourself, "Maybe I *didn't* see or hear that." Though perspectives can be changed, reality can't be. You'll feel as if something is off, that they aren't right somehow, but because they've convinced you it isn't, you accept it. Deep down though, you know it's not true.

Lemon Solution #18: When encountering gaslighting, be it with family, friends, or co-workers, trust your gut and your instincts. If someone is trying to tell you something happened a certain way and you know for sure it didn't, don't accept their version of events. Stand firm. If you are repeatedly experiencing gaslighting, especially in work relationships, try documenting the situation. By having documentation it's no longer your word against theirs because you have evidence to add substance to your claims.

Name-calling: Gottlieb, the famous social scientist that accurately predicted which couples would stay together and which ones wouldn't, created a high-quality test for relationship endurance. His term for these was, "the four horsemen of the apocalypse," or the end of the relationship. This includes contempt. Contempt is defined as something or someone that is beneath consideration or respect. In the context of a relationship, this spells doom. And name-calling is a huge sign of contempt. When you were a child, you may have engaged in name-calling. It often was a signal of your immaturity and inability to express frustration and anger. However, as you grew older, you began to learn better ways of communicating your feelings, especially to those you loved, respected, and admired.

However, when you are an adult and someone you are in a relationship with, whether platonic or not, engages in verbally cutting you down, it is a sign of blatant disrespect. It is also a failing on their part. Instead of them being able to tell you in a tactful way how they feel, they construct a way instead to make you feel horrible about yourself. That's not love, and it certainly isn't respect.

Being dismissive: Has anyone ever told you "You're too sensitive," or "You're overreacting." How did that make you feel? It probably made you feel as if you *were* being that way, but it also minimized your feelings and possibly made you feel small. By dismissing your valid points, a toxic person doesn't have to deal with them. They can just shrug off your concerns and make you look as if you're being too emotional or overreacting. The truth is, you are entitled to your feelings. You are also entitled to being listened to.

Not taking accountability: I once had a friend that was in an emotionally abusive relationship. Her husband of six years was cheating on her. When she found out, he turned it around on her and told her, "Well, I did it because you..." She ended up feeling as if the affair was her fault, even though deep down she knew it wasn't true. After finally getting the healing she needed, she separated from her husband and took control of her life.

When someone does you wrong, they should make amends. We are familiar with love languages but are unaware that people have specific ways that they need to receive an apology. There are several apology languages which include expressing regret, accepting responsibility, making restitution, genuine repentance, and requesting forgiveness. Not taking responsibility allows the toxic person to deflect their behaviors onto another person. It allows them to say, "Hey, I'm not the bad guy here." But the truth is, if they are wrong, they should apologize and try to never repeat the action or behavior again. If someone you love is engaging in this, you may want to rethink your relationship with them. You deserve to be around people that are responsible and accountable for the things they say and do.

Using money or other resources as control: This is a huge factor in many toxic relationships. You could experience this with a romantic partner, a parent or guardian, or even a friend. Money as control is a way to keep someone from leaving a bad situation. Saying, "If you go, you won't be able to have this or that..." is enough of a deterrent for many people in today's world to stay where they aren't happy. It's a harsh world and having financial security and state of mind make things better and easier.

However, having the constant fear that money or resources will be taken away if the toxic person isn't pleased can be a horrible way to live. Living in peace is often a better way than to stay in a situation or relationship where you have to act accordingly or lose something like money or much needed services, including medical care.

Lemon Solution #19: If you find yourself in a situation where money is being used as a means of control, there is a way out. There are tons of programs out there designed to help people to leave a controlling situation, and with today's expanding economy, it is easier than ever to make money on the side to save and then eventually leave. If you want to get out, you need to begin to set a plan in motion. For more details, see the chapter on financial lemons.

Physical abuse: If someone is hitting you, punching you or slapping you — THAT IS NEVER OKAY! It doesn't matter if you and the person you are with have been together for years. It doesn't matter if the person is a relative or friend. Physical abuse is never right. If you are afraid to leave or speak up, there are valuable resources online where you can get sound advice on how to protect yourself. In many states, there are emergency protective orders you can get as an abuse victim within a matter of 24 hours or so. Police are often trained to handle domestic disputes and can make sure you're safe while you gather your things and leave.

Lemon Solution #20: If you are experiencing abuse of any kind, call the National Abuse Hotline: 1-800-799-7233 or the Substance Abuse and Mental Health Hotline: 1-800-662-HELP (4357). If you are dealing with suicidal ideations, call the National Suicide Hotline at 1-800-273-8255.

We often find ourselves at the mercy of family, friends and co-workers that are just as toxic and emotionally (or even physically) abusive. Give yourself permission to not have a relationship with that person. In the end, a toxic person's way of life isn't your responsibility. If you've ever been in this kind of relationship, it's time to stop blaming yourself. Toxic people hone their skills over many years; it's not an overnight phenomenon. They study you and everyone around you in order to use what they can see to get what they want. Take the relationship as a lesson for the future instead. Understand that even though you were a part of their lives, you had no control over who they chose to be.

We may often feel that it is our duty to put up with an aunt that constantly berates and puts us down, or even a parent that makes us feel as if we are less than. You don't have to. Live life for yourself, and build happy, healthy relationships with the people around you. Set boundaries and train people the way you want them to treat you. We have to decide when enough is enough, how much toxic lemonade you're willing to drink before realizing that you're ready to choose health and, most importantly, to choose yourself.

It's Okay to be Vulnerable

As we touched on earlier, some lemons are complete surprises, and there is nothing that can be done about it until the lemon is in front of you. Two such lemons are sickness and death. Though these are extreme lemons, they're real and require a level of vulnerability that most are uncomfortable with. I have experienced both of these bitter lemons, and I imagine that many of you have too. These two lemons are some of the bitterest to swallow, but that doesn't mean they can't be overcome.

In the home stretch of completing *When Life Gives You Lemons...Stop Making Lemonade*, my mother went into the hospital. Her heart rate was low, and I was really scared and concerned for her. At the same time, I was also worried about what would happen with the book because I was relying on getting the book to publication on time. I was so dedicated to trying to both be there for my mom and meet deadlines that I had my computer with me in the hospital! I spoke with my editor and graphic designer/marketing consultant to let them know what was going on and we worked everything out, so we didn't get behind.

When going through unexpected tests, we often tend to isolate and try and bear the burden on our own. This is often done under the guise of accountability and responsibility. Responsibility and taking ownership require open, transparent communication with those you are working with. Sometimes you can't handle lemons of sickness by yourself, but those around you may have the tools to pick up the slack for a short period of time. Thankfully, my mom got better and was discharged from the hospital.

We live in a society that rewards strength and courage. We are inspired by stories of those who have overcome obstacles and adversities to become champions. We cry along with our favorite stars when they've received a hard-won award. We identify with strength. We embrace and celebrate it. What we don't always care for is the process. We never see what goes on behind the scenes.

We'd like to think that there is some magical way of coming through obstacles without a scratch. We are often taught to ignore the process and aim for the result. But you can't get from point A to point C without something in between. There must be something other the beginning and the end. When someone is going through a crisis, we don't want to see the tears, the anger, and the pain.

That's too sensitive for most people. In an age where anything and everything goes, we're troubled by the process of getting from a place of hurt and loss to getting to a place where there's strength and peace. We tell those who are depressed to get over it. We medicate them. When someone is diagnosed with cancer and manages to beat it back, we tell them, "You are so brave. You are so courageous!"

We don't tell them, "All those days you spent in chemotherapy, sick, losing hair, being vulnerable, and just wanting for it all to be over, I can understand that must have been a hard process. You aren't alone. Let me know if you need any support or want to talk." No one says these things. We think it's rude. Ironically, we think it shows that we don't care.

What it really shows is that we are afraid. We are afraid to be vulnerable. For us to get to the strength part, the part that is wrapped in ribbons and taken to dinner parties and touted in speeches across the country is true vulnerability. We have to be taken down to our most basic parts and allow the natural processes to take hold before we can move forward. And it isn't always pretty.

People diagnosed with serious illnesses aren't always brave. Sometimes they're angry. Hurt. Feeling as if it's unfair. They may rail, scream, and cry. And it's only the aftermath, the result of diligent care and treatment, that we see the results. This is why we whisper, "You are so brave." We don't always give ourselves permission to be vulnerable.

We don't give others that same latitude either. What are we so afraid of? Why is it that we are afraid to be...not okay? We think that if we are not okay, then something must be wrong. We feel that to be completely human is somehow not good enough. Perhaps we feel that if we're are in a sensitive place it means that we are weak. But that's not the case at all. If you are allowing yourself the chance to be vulnerable, you are giving yourself permission. And that in and of itself is a hard choice. It is one that takes incredible determination and strength. Sometimes it takes a really strong-minded individual to say, "I'm not doing my best today. Things are tough. I need help and support."

We think that if we say these things, it means that we aren't taking care of what our duties are. We have to smile, say thank you when we're told we're brave, and not show a single tear. We're expected to be this way no matter how tough it is. I remember watching a program where a super tough, no-nonsense life coach was helping a single mother whose husband had passed away suddenly. They had been high-school sweethearts and had been very much in love up until the day he'd died. I was watching the program with friends of mine. The program was upbeat and very much "Let's get your life back in order!" complete with an up-tempo music track and smiling helpers who cleaned the house, got the finances back on track, and even a fitness coach to get the mom back in shape.

What gave my friends and I pause was the uncomfortable moment when the mom broke down. She let out soul-wrenching, heartrending sobs and yelled, "Why did you leave me?! I just feel so alone. He left me. He was supposed to be here with me. Why did he die?" She was airing out her sadness and her inability to just go on without acknowledging the importance her husband had in her life.

The host was extremely uncomfortable, I could tell. My friends fidgeted and watched with a sort of embarrassed kind of sympathy, as if they couldn't bear to think that this woman wasn't okay. Some even excused themselves to go get water, snacks or the like from the kitchen. I remember thinking to myself, *"She needs to get it together. She'll be fine. She just has to work at it."*

I didn't understand the woman's pain until it happened to me. My father passed away when I was 19 years old. It was the hardest time in my life. I couldn't imagine my dad not being there. He'd always been there. It was like having the very foundations of a house being pulled away. Everything tumbled down. Everything felt as if it had lost meaning. I got the well-wishes, and the "I'm so sorry, for your loss," spiel. People patted my back and shoulders and I gave them sad smiles, hosted parties, said toasts, and worked to make everyone feel comfortable.

I didn't want people to think I wasn't strong. I didn't want people to think I wasn't okay. But I wasn't. I quickly spiraled into a depression and told no one for a very long time. I felt as if I needed to show everyone, including my own family, that I was fine. After all, I was young and had a bright future ahead of me. And death happens every day, right? Someone dies every moment we're alive, so it's expected. I'd smile and tell my mom, "I'm okay. Let's talk about you." Or I'd quickly change the subject when friends would ask or say, "Yeah, it's tough. But I'm moving forward." The result was that people really thought I was okay. I went back to work. I went back to school. I hung out with my friends. I visited family. The whole time, I wasn't okay. I felt all wrong. I felt out of whack. I didn't find pleasure in life anymore.

It began to hurt to smile. It hurt to pretend. But I tried. I tried so hard that each day became a battle. Get up and let them know you're fine. Give a rousing mini speech on how you're getting over it. Laugh. Talk. Have wine. Make plans. Go home. Break down. Think about not living anymore because the pain is so great. Wash, rinse, repeat.

It was a very close friend of mine who came to visit one day, and while I was merrily going about the house, fixing cups of tea and setting out cookies and making her feel at home, she put down her mug and said to me, "You're not okay." "Oh no!" I insisted. "I'm just fine." She calmly informed me that she knew I wasn't. She reached out to me and gave me a hug. "I don't know what it's like to lose a parent, but I do know what it's like to lose someone you're close to, and I know you're not okay. You're down. It hurts and that's okay. It's okay to be that way."

I tried to smile, but it hurt too much. I began to cry, and I couldn't stop. She listened; she held my hands. She hugged me. She gave me tissues. She didn't offer platitudes. She simply helped me to cry. After that, I got help. I went to a therapist, and they helped me to navigate my grief. I told my mother and my family. I wasn't surprised to find that they weren't okay either. We made a pact to be vulnerable with each other, to not pretend. That's when the true healing began. Through the tears and late-night talks, we began to see dad again. Not just the fact that he was gone, but what he provided when he was alive. We'd talk about how much we missed him, and we'd remember things we'd forgotten. We recognized that his death had left a hole that could never be filled and that was okay.

It's okay to talk about those who've passed away who had an impact on our lives. It's okay to cry and feel it's unfair that they are not in our lives anymore. It's okay to feel vulnerable. It's okay to feel like there are some days you just want to stay in bed because getting up means facing a life without the person you love. It's okay to admit you need help.

We all cried together. We all talked together. We all healed together. I'm never going to stop missing my dad. It will be an ache that will be with me forever. It hurts even now when I see my child and he does or says something my dad would have done, or I look at my son and realize he looks just like him. It hurts all over again sometimes. But I've learned that it's okay. I give myself permission to feel that way, and each day, each moment hurts less than the last. You may think to yourself, "Well, maybe it's better to not love at all," but that's not the answer.

We all need to be connected to others in order to thrive. Healthy relationships are essential. Sure, we could live like hermits, but I'm sure not all of us would be happy that way. Our lives are given meaning when we can spend time with others, exchange ideas and feelings and yes, love them. Also, I think in order to love, we have to be vulnerable.

I also think vulnerability is honesty. When you're vulnerable, you're honest with yourself about how you feel. You're honest with those around you. You're seeing who you are unfiltered. That's necessary. It's the only way that we truly become our most authentic selves. Even when we fall in love, we have to be vulnerable. Love isn't just about saying "I love you." It sometimes means being vulnerable with another person and that's scary. It really is. You have to be your most honest self with someone who may leave or hurt you.

However, love is about honesty and openness, and when you are open to receiving and giving love, you have a stronger and better relationship. A friend of mine once told me that her husband chased her for over a year. I asked her why, as he seemed charming, was good-looking, and they genuinely seemed to be in love.

She told me something that gave me pause. She said she didn't want to get hurt, and she knew she'd fall for him. So, for her, it was easier to push him away, even though no one else she was going out with made her happy. Think about that. She was willing to stay in the same place, being unhappy rather than run the risk of getting hurt. It would seem more logical that she should open up and find love and being even *happier*, than to just stay in the same place.

She ended up finally going out with him nearly a year and a half later. They had one date, then another, and then another still. He was kind, engaging and just—everything she had ever wanted. By the time they were on their tenth date, she knew he was the one. They went out for four years, moved in together, and got married soon after. She is now happily married with a little girl that is five-months old. When she finally made the decision to be vulnerable, she said it was extremely hard. "But it was rewarding," I remember her saying. "I bargained but got more than what I expected."

She told me that the first few months she was with him, she was fearful. He wanted to get to know her, and she felt as if she had to keep her guard up. He tried and tried to get past her defenses. Finally, he confronted her about it. She hadn't even realized what she was doing until she sat down and thought about it. She had been hurt in prior relationships by people that hadn't meant well, and she was afraid that this wonderful man would do the same thing. She began by confessing her fears to him, and then he did something she hadn't expected: he told her he felt the same way.

She was surprised. She hadn't thought that he would feel the same way. After all, he seemed so confident, loving, and sweet. He was afraid as well, but he'd put his fears aside and let himself be vulnerable. It allowed him the luxury of letting her get to know him, and he hoped she would do the same. It was then that her walls came down. Their romance wasn't perfect, but it was filled with the kind of love she'd always dreamt of having. "And to think," she told me, "I would have never been with him if I hadn't let my guard down and just let myself be vulnerable."

To be fair, being vulnerable *does* carry some risk. You don't know if the person you have entrusted will hurt you or betray you. However, if you think you won't be able to get over the hurt or the feeling that it will leave you, think again. We have the capacity as human beings to learn from our experiences and choose wisely the next time we have the same opportunity. Our brains are also wired to bounce back. We've been created to go through adversity and triumph. But we just have to let ourselves feel as if it's okay to be honest with others and ourselves. We too often think it puts us at a disadvantage if we're vulnerable.

A lot of people spend their lives closed off and unhappy. They think if they could just keep people at arm's length, they will be just fine. The truth is, we all yearn to feel connected. We all yearn to feel as if we matter to someone. That is never anything to be ashamed of. It is what makes us human.

Lemon Solution #21: Sickness and death are two bitter lemons that you don't always know what to do with. They come suddenly, and their bitterness lingers. There is no clear-cut solution, only that you need to give yourself space and time to process. Time may not heal all things, but it helps give you time to process. Focus on the memories and lessons you gained from their life. Allow those things to give you the propulsion you need to move forward but always remember their legacy.

This chapter features two lemon drops that address two scenarios that arise when dealing with the relationships in your life. Sometimes sitting down and hashing things out over a nice dessert is all that is needed to restore peace and harmony. If you think that's the best approach for your situation (or if you are just craving dessert) see page 65 for a Sweet Lemon Treat. However, often our relationships ring us dry, causing us to lose our shine. If you need to get the shine back in your life, check out the practical tip on lemon's whitening properties on page 67.

Sweet Lemon Treat: *Magic Lemon Cups*

This recipe serves between 6-8 individuals. Total preparation time is about 1 hour.

Ingredients:

- 1 cup sugar
- 2 tablespoons unsalted butter, softened
- 5 tablespoons fresh lemon juice, & the zest of 1 lemon
- 1/4 cup of all-purpose flour
- Pinch of salt
- 3 large eggs, separated
- 1 ½ cups milk

Instructions: Heat the oven to 350 degrees. Place six to eight small ramekins at the bottom of a 9- by 13-inch cake pan. In a large bowl, beat together the sugar and butter with an electric mixer until the butter is fully incorporated. Beat in the lemon juice, lemon zest, flour and salt. In a small bowl, whisk together the egg yolks. Beat the egg yolks into the sugar mixture, followed by the milk. Clean the mixer beaters.

In a second large bowl, beat the egg whites with the electric mixer on medium-low speed until frothy, about 1 minute. Increase the speed to medium-high and continue to beat until the eggs form stiff peaks, 3 to 5 minutes. Transfer about one-quarter of the egg whites to the sugar mixture and stir gently to incorporate. Gently fold the remaining egg whites into the sugar mixture; it is okay if some of the egg whites remain visible.

Divide the batter between the ramekins. Place the cake pan, with the ramekins inside, on the center rack of the oven. Carefully pour water into the cake pan, around the ramekins, until it reaches about halfway up the sides of the ramekins. Bake until the cake is firm and light golden brown, 35 to 40 minutes.

Carefully transfer the ramekins to a cooling rack and let sit at least until the ramekins are cool enough to handle. Serve warm or at room temperature. (If you would like to flip the cakes out so that the pudding is on top, wait until the cakes are completely cooled. Run a knife around the inside of the ramekin, place a small dessert plate on top of the cake, and flip over to release the cake. If necessary, tap firmly on the bottom of the ramekin to dislodge any stubborn bits.) The cakes are best eaten the day they are baked.

Source: Southern Kitchen

Sweet Lemon Treat: *Lemon Whitening Aid*

Ingredients:
- 2 lemons
- One gallon of hot water

Instructions: Take about 1/2 cup lemon juice and mix with one gallon of very hot water. Soak the clothes in the mixture overnight. If you're in a rush, soak it at least for an hour. However, the dirtier the clothes, the more it will benefit from a nice, long soak. Do not use for silk, it is best for cotton and polyester. Carefully remove your clothing from the mixture and pour the remaining mixture into the washing machine. Launder as usual. A great thing about lemons is that you can't over-bleach!

Lemon Lessons:

- 🍋 It doesn't matter what type of "ship" you're in, you are the captain and able to determine whether you capsize.

- 🍋 Abusive relationships are NEVER okay! Find safe, but expedient ways to get out of a dangerous situation.

- 🍋 Are you the toxic, abusive person? Learn to recognize the harm that you are doing to others and seek the help you need to eradicate those behaviors.

- 🍋 Remember that you cannot control how others perceive you, but the company you keep is often a good indicator of how you see yourself.

- 🍋 Vulnerability is necessary for healthy relationships, and it also allows you to heal from life's bitter lemons.

Lemon Checkpoint:

- Are the relationships in your life beneficial or draining you?
- How are you going to affirm yourself and not succumb to other's abusive behavior?
- Do you give yourself space to be vulnerable, and deal with the lemons that take you by surprise?

When Life Gives You Lemons...Stop Making Lemonade

Chapter 4

Professional Lemons

> **Lemon Drop:** *It may sound like a science fiction, but lemons can be used to make—a battery! That's right. You don't have to be MacGyver (remember him?) to jimmy one up. You can make a lemon battery with just a lemon and two metallic electrodes such as a penny and a galvanized nail. The battery is not exactly powered from the lemon, but from the changes that occur on a chemical level in the zinc from the galvanized nail. The lemon juice acts on the nail and oxidizes and releases some of its latent energy. A single lemon can generate up to .9 volts of electricity! You can use multiple lemons and triple the output. To try this out, turn to page 91 for instructions.*

C hapter 3 touched on relationship lemons and how toxicity can spoil the lemonade. One relationship that takes up a lot of time that we don't often consider a relationship is our jobs. When you think about it, depending on the job, you may spend more time at work than with your family and friends. Due to how much time we spend at work, it's crucial for our well-being to have our professional lemons in order.

Missed Promotion

After working in corporate America for over 16 years, I've witnessed all types of lemons in the workplace. Seeing the lemons people diluted and made into lemonade opened my eyes to my own sour points. One series of lemons I dealt with started when I returned from maternity leave. I was getting back in the groove of sales and making my mark again. A leadership opportunity became available, and I was more than qualified for the position. I put together a glamourous transition plan with my resume laced with all the key words. I interviewed and made it all the way to the final round before they told me they were hiring someone else from another company.

That was a big sour blow. What made it even more sour was I was tasked to help train this new leader. That really hurt because it said to me that I wasn't good enough to have the job, but I was good enough to support and ramp up this individual that has no idea of the internal systems and programs. So, what did I do? Diluted this lemon and made lemonade. I smiled, sipped my lemonade, and supported my new teammate. This went on for about nine months, and then the new leader quit. Now the job was posted again, and surely, I would be the ideal candidate. Not only was I qualified, but I had sipped patiently on my lemonade as I helped train the new person and pleased all parties.

It's round two of the interviews, and the candidate pool went from 60 to 30 to 15 to 5 to 2 then to only ME. After five grueling rounds of interviews, I was the last one standing. My confidence was high, I felt great! This was my moment to grow in my leadership career. I was preparing my 30-60-90 transition plan. I wanted this to be a seamless and effective progression. I was prepared and ready to unify the teams and increase production.

I got the call to have a meeting with the executive. I took a big refreshing gulp of the lemonade that I had been making from my lemons with the last disappointment of not getting the job. Self-assured, I walked into the office. The conversation started with, "Leesa you are valuable here, you work so hard and we appreciate your commitment to the company and your peers BUT we have decided to repost the job." At that moment, I felt like someone kicked me in the gut. I was in such disbelief and shock that I just started to sob uncontrollably. I felt like I was stood up at the altar. The feeling when you think you are in love and the person loves you just as much, but when it's time to make a public declaration of your commitment to each other, you get blindsided and rejected. This was just as humiliating because EVERYONE knew I was the last candidate, and I was essentially doing the job. Each day going to work was a constant reminder I was rejected after I put myself out there for a second time. The fact that they just reposted the job made it even more deflating.

With lemons galore surrounding my thoughts and life, I quickly fell into a victim state of mind. I began getting angry and was starting to withdraw from everyone. One day I had an epiphany. Why am I allowing this job to dictate my happiness? I needed to stop making lemonade and figure out what was causing the sour points. I had to have some tough conversations and self-assessments.

I wasn't going to take these sour points and just pacify things by making more lemonade. I wanted to find the root causes. I needed to find out why I was qualified for a job and good enough to execute the duties involved while they were looking for a replacement, but not the choice for the actual role. I looked in the mirror and realized I had to take supreme accountability and figure out my lemons. I asked for feedback and started to read some leadership development books. A few of my favorites are *Extreme Ownership: How U.S. Navy SEALs Lead and Win*, by Jocko Willink and Leif Babin, *Start with Why* by Simon Sinek, and *The Success Principles* by Jack Canfield.

All these books shared valuable information on how to own your life and take control of your narrative. I did that, I joined Toastmasters, and worked on growing myself. The feedback I received was that I was "too nice." I decided to take my sparkly unicorn image and transform myself into a stallion. I was still true to who I was at the core but learned to temper my bubbly personality and allow people to earn the privilege to know the fun, outgoing, version of me. I began to put myself in situations that were uncomfortable and challenge myself, such as competing in the World Championship for Public Speaking.

The more I faced my lemons, the more my professional career exploded. I got a promotion for a different leadership role that provided me with a more global view. I was able to collaborate with leaders from various departments. It was better than I could even imagine. People started to notice my shift and began to pattern their behavior after mine.

Lemon Solution #22: Being passed over at work is a horrible feeling. If you see this is a recurring problem, begin to ask for 360 feedback, and conduct a S.W.O.T. analysis of your own performance. A S.W.O.T. analysis is a tool that measures Strengths, Weaknesses, Opportunities, and Threats. Though this is typically a business metric, don't be afraid to apply it to your own life to help chart your professional development.

Don't Be Afraid to Negotiate

I f you see that you are qualified, yet still being passed over for job opportunities, don't be afraid to advocate for yourself! Negotiate! Women especially sometimes have an issue with this because of a fear of how they will be perceived. This is no time for fear! Stop making lemonade! Stop swallowing your emotions and your ambition and throw your hat in the ring. You are qualified, you are enough! The same goes for making sure that you are being paid properly for your work. There's a saying in business that no one will ever pay you what you're worth. If you find that to be untenable, do something about it and negotiate the rate you deserve, or at least the rate you can live with.

A friend of mine, Terri, once told me a story of how she became so successful in her career. She was an award-winning Hollywood heavyweight, and worked for some of the hottest men and women in the industry. She didn't get there overnight, but she learned some valuable lessons along the way. She told me a story once about her first couple of clients. They weren't very well known but had deep pockets. She had just gotten into the public relations and communication industry and was eager to prove her worth.

Terri was willing to work for cheap and nearly free. She was hoping to undercut her competition and prove that she was okay with cutting her teeth and growing her brand. What ended up happening was that she ended up doing a great job, working day and night and boosting her client's profile for – little or nothing. There's a fine line between doing something for exposure and cutting yourself off at the knees.

Word began to get around that she was a great media and communications expert and she was cheap! That was virtually unheard of in the industry. Terri soon found herself fielding intricate and demanding requests that were below market value. She was working hard, cobbling together projects and clients for little to no money. She finally had had enough and decided that she now that she had proven her worth, she needed to charge accordingly.

Sure, she experienced a decline in clients, but she gained clients that were willing to meet her price and then some. The ones she was able to retain realized that her services were valuable. Finding good help these days is hard, and people who understand this concept are willing to pay. Terri began to refuse jobs that didn't suit her needs, and she found that though she wasn't as busy as before, she wasn't overwhelmed.

Terri also let me in on a little secret: when people feel that they are getting a great service for cheap or free, they will place **more** demands on you, not less. She told about an organization she was a consultant for many years ago. She had settled for a low salary out of desperation and looking back on it, says she should have been concerned when the company head was so happy that she accepted their offer. They were ecstatic because they were getting a great worker for a very low price. She was afraid to negotiate or walk away because she didn't think she could find anything better. She learned quickly that many in her field weren't accepting a certain salary and that she shouldn't either. Terri was quickly burned out in that position as she worked tirelessly and had little pay to back her up. She soon went job hunting and found something more suitable.

She was determined to negotiate. They made an offer she didn't quite like and she countered. They accepted. It was that simple! She was floored. All those years she was working for scraps and she could have negotiated her price? It may seem pretty simple, but many people devalue their worth out of desperation and fear. Don't ever be afraid to negotiate, to stand by the price of your services and the value you're bringing to a job or client.

Lemon Solution #23: The first step to successful negotiation is understand your industry or field. You want to be sure that the services you are providing are on par with the average. Research what leaders in the industry are doing and what others are pricing for their services. It may be tempting to "undercut" the competition, but you also don't want to cut your own bottom-line and profit margin. Become knowledgeable about the reasonable expectations of those working in your field, and don't settle for less!

Changing Perceptions and The Chameleon Effect Revisited

Sometimes, you are the reason that you are unable to negotiate properly and move forward. As I shared with you a bit earlier, I was passed over for a promotion that I was qualified for because I was perceived as being too nice. It was from this experience that I realized; I didn't like being a people pleaser. Not only was I short-changing myself, I was short-changing others as well. I was giving people what I thought they wanted and not a true exchange of ideas and values.

There was a time when I decided to tell a colleague of mine how I really felt about their idea and gave them suggestions that I thought would fit with what they were looking for. I was hesitant because I was sure they would be offended. The reverse was true. They wanted a genuine, honest and informed opinion. I was being my truest self and engaged in a professional courtesy that they appreciated wholeheartedly. In fact, they pulled me to the side and told me, "I am grateful you were being honest with me. I asked a few people and they said go ahead, but when I talked to you, your suggestions made me realize I needed to tweak a few things. I did the presentation and it was a success. Thanks for your help!" I felt so good after hearing that! The old me would have just said, "Hey, this is great!" while holding back honest feedback. From this experience I realized I could still be a wonderful, warm person and not be a people pleaser.

I started small. Acquaintances would suggest a restaurant and instead of going along with everything, I'd say things like, "Hey, there's a new restaurant down the street. I'd love to try that. Would you all be open to it?" I started actively participating in meetings and speaking up. I began to define myself for myself. I didn't hesitate anymore but took leaps of faith. I had to give myself mini pep talks at times, but I persisted in making this change. I would be so wrapped up in pleasing people that I often found that I was diminishing myself. Not only that, there was no reciprocity. I was going out of my way for people; they gave an inch while I gave a mile, and I knew that I could no longer continue without my behavior becoming detrimental to my personal and professional growth.

I began learning an incredible lesson: you can't control everything. Not even how people perceive you, regardless if it is positive or negative, or how they think or move through the world. The only thing you can control is your reaction. Sometimes our reactions to the things we can't control help us immensely in other areas of our lives. For example, I once had a boss that would always come to work in the later hours of the morning. I was always the first person in the office. I'm not sure why she began to grow suspicious, but she suddenly began to claim that I was coming into the office at later times and leaving early.

I was shocked. How could she say such a thing? I wondered. After all, I came in before she did! I didn't think I could defend myself. I didn't clock in and out like other employees had to as I was salaried, but I knew that I had kept good hours, even coming in early and leaving late sometimes! I gathered my evidence: emails I had sent from my desk when I had just come in, projects and people I had met with during the early morning hours, and even logs of packages I had signed for when they came into our department very early in the morning.

I then made a practice of emailing my boss from my desk each time I was in the office to let her know I was working. I made sure that I did a round about the office floor so that others could see me and know I was there, rather than being stuck away in my cubicle. I became very organized with my work and kept track of everything I did during the day and what times I did it. When I had a mandatory meeting with my boss and HR about my supposed tardiness, my boss was embarrassed when I pulled up the evidence. She claimed that she had somehow gotten bad information from another member of our team. She said that the member had tried to find me during a company-wide PR crisis. The supposed person couldn't find me at my cubicle and just assumed I hadn't come in yet. She apologized and said she'd be careful next time with what information she gave credence to and that she'd do her due diligence with those kinds of claims in the future.

After that, I made it a practice to become very organized and aware of my time. I also kept track of emails, conversations, and other things, and this led me to become a better employee over time. After a time, my boss was let go and replaced with someone else. I ended up working at another company sometime later, but my habits became ingrained. These habits enabled me to become a more conscientious worker and I was promoted six months into working at the newer position.

Though I couldn't change my old boss and her actions, I could change and mold my own. Her actions prompted me to see my own lemon and decide what to do with it. I was able to take that lemon and create something wonderful that aided myself and others down the road. You can't always control the random things that happen in life, but you certainly can use those moments to not only react in a way that gives you power, but in a way that lays the foundation for you to have better habits in the future.

If I had been content to continue being a people pleaser, I never would have gathered the evidence necessary to advocate for myself. I also wouldn't have been adding true value to my team, instead of hiding behind what I perceived to be politically correct answers. I learned that you can be honest without creating a whirlwind or backlash. Studies have shown that if you want a profitable business, being aware of your employees emotional needs makes a difference.

Emotional Intelligence

Unfortunately, many companies value intelligence (IG) over emotional intelligence (EQ). This preference for IQ over EQ is based upon a company's values. If the company values money as its priority, then they may not be as concerned about EQ. Studies have shown however that if you want to have a profitable business, you need to be aware of the emotional needs of your employees. Of course, there is a time and place for everything, and work should not become therapy or a place of oversharing (unless of course you are a therapist), but a bit of empathy goes a long way. There are five components of Emotional Intelligence—let's break them down.

Self-Awareness: Self-awareness requires you to be in touch with your strengths and weaknesses. You can identify how you come across to others and manage yourself based on who else is in the room. To be self-aware is related to being adaptable. The benefit of being self-aware in the workplace is that as a manager, you have the wisdom of adding members to your team that are strong in the areas that you're not. An egotistical manager always wants to feel superior. A wise manager wants a balanced, well-rounded team. Being self-aware also helps you receive feedback. If you are unable to receive constructive feedback, you risk ending your career prematurely.

Lemon Solution #24: To increase your self-awareness, keep a record of feedback received in order to see if there are any through lines. Also, pay attention to how people react to you, and how you react to others, especially in situations where you have felt triggered.

Self-Regulation: This is your ability to gauge which response is most appropriate given the situation. It's the ability to think before you speak. Often, work environments test you in ways that make you want to forget yourself. You can't do that if you want to maintain a peaceful work environment, whether you are the boss or the employee. This is also especially important for entrepreneurs and freelancers. If you have a client-facing business and struggle with self-regulation, check out the lemon solution below.

Lemon Solution #25: To improve your communication, try deep breathing to ensure that your response is tone appropriate. Also remember that emails can be tone deaf. If annoyed, take a few moments to gather yourself before responding to an email. When possible also gather the input of others. If you still fear that you came across incorrectly, don't be afraid to follow up with a phone call or face-to-face meeting.

Empathy: Empathy is often mistaken for sympathy, and they are not the same thing. Sympathy is feelings of sorrow or pity for someone else's situation. Empathy however is being able to imagine yourself in someone else's situation without ever having experienced it. People often try to keep empathy out of the office because they feel that it opens people to being too "emotional" at work. We are not automatons, and it's better for the business when employees are able to bring their entire selves to work instead of having to compartmentalize. Employees will respect you more, and perform better, if they feel that you care. You also will gain a better understanding of why members of your team behave as they do.

Lemon Solution #26: If you struggle with empathy, work on your active listening skills. Active listening includes listening to understand, not to respond. Active listening also means to not interrupt. Another way to increase your empathy is to not ignore the emotions of those around you. If you see someone is upset, don't put your blinders on; address it instead.

Motivation: To be motivated is to move past obstacles to continue your professional growth. If you're not motivated, it will show in your performance and could be an indicator that you need to be doing something else.

Lemon Solution #27: If you aren't motivated at work, consider ways for you to approach your work differently so that you can find enjoyment in it. Also try renewed goal setting. If this doesn't work, don't be afraid to find a new career that better aligns with your goals and current lifestyle.

Social Skills: The final component of Emotional Intelligence is social skills. Part of making it in the corporate or business world is being able to network effectively. This is also being able to pick up on social cues such as sarcasm and jokes.

Lemon Solution #28: Networking and social skills can be difficult for introverts. However, it can be worked through by finding a communication and networking style that best suits your reserved personality. Extroverts, take into consideration the introverts on your team. Too often introverts are expected to come out of their shells to meet the engagement of levels of extroverts. This can lead to burn out. Instead, try creating a quieter, less charged workplace, for a change of pace.

Cultural Competency

L inked to emotional intelligence is the concept of cultural competency. We live and work in a diverse society and so there is no time or place for discrimination of any kind. Someone without emotional intelligence is going to have a very difficult time creating a culturally competent workplace. To be culturally competent, as stated by *Make It Our Business*, one must:

- Be aware of one's own worldview.
- Develop positive attitudes towards cultural differences.
- Gain knowledge of different cultural practices and worldviews.
- Develop skills for communication and interaction across cultures and demographics.

There are four generations that make up the majority of workplace, Baby Boomers, Generation X, Millennials, and Generation Z. These four groups have different needs, tastes, and sensibilities. It's important to not participate in ageist behaviors, regardless of if it's directed towards someone older or younger. Instead work to understand the generational differences to create a cohesive team. You have to go beyond just being tolerant, though that's a start. It's important to identify and counter biases you may have that could create a hostile workplace for someone else.

An associate shared with me how she practices cultural competency at work. She works as a college professor and teaches African American Studies. Though her students are predominantly African American, she does have a multicultural classroom. She was explaining to me how it is important to her to not alter the course material in order to not diminish any of the realities of the experiences of African Americans in North America. However, she structures the lectures in a way that invites *all* students, not just those who identify as African American, to determine how their worldviews impact the way they perceive "the other," and how they may also other themselves.

As highlighted above, cultural competency requires intentionality. Having a workplace that promotes this is extremely important to me because I have mixed heritage. I have been in workplaces where people, unsure of my ethnicity, would make snide, demeaning remarks about African Americans or Asians. Imagine their surprise when I let them know that their comments were personally offensive. You never want to get caught in that type of situation. Especially with the rate at which people change jobs, you never know where the colleague you insulted may end up next. They may end up as the gatekeeper for the position you want next.

Lemon Solution #29: If you find that your diverse workplace isn't gelling the way it needs to, try attending the events held by the different diversity groups at your office. If your office doesn't have these, make it a point to get to know your co-workers. Ask (appropriate) questions and actively work to dispel stereotypes and biases.

R-E-S-P-E-C-T!

A retha Franklin said it best: "R-E-S-P-E-C-T, find out what it means to me!" Everything that we have talked about up to now points directly to respect. Respect is crucial not just in the workplace but in life. Some of the biggest lemons come from seeds of disrespect. Too many of us live life with the mindset "You have to give respect to get it." While it would be nice for respect to be reciprocal amongst parties, the reality is that this isn't always the case. Just because someone is disrespectful to you doesn't mean you need to do the same. You need to count the cost and see if going tit for tat is really best for your career or well-being. I'd like to offer you a challenge geared towards helping you gain and maintain respect.

Self-Respect: Determine if you are showing others that you respect yourself enough to expect respect in return. You attract what you put into the universe.

Don't fear the rebuilding process: Sometimes you hit rock bottom. That's okay as long as you don't stay there. If you have lost self-respect, be honest with yourself as to when and why. Once you address these two points, you can then begin to put in the work to get back to where you were, and then on to where you want to be.

Accept your mistakes: We are human and therefore we are going to mess up. Don't try and hide your mistakes. Instead, take ownership and get to the root of the problem. People are going to begin noticing if you're always coming up with lemonade instead of results. Work through what you need to, and take note of what happened because the best apology is changed behavior.

Keep your eye on the prize: People will respect you, and you will respect yourself, if you are unapologetic about the direction in which you are walking. People may not always agree with your vision, but they will respect you for having something that you're working toward.

Recognize that building self-respect is a process: Respect can be lost in an instant, and it takes time to rebuild. Don't allow the fact that it can be a daunting process keep you from putting in the necessary work.

Professional lemons don't have to be disastrous. Sometimes, you just need a reset and to change out your battery. If that's you, take a look at how lemons can be used as a source of battery power.

Sweet Lemon Treat: *Lemon Powered Battery*

Ingredients:

- Two lemons
- A sharp knife
- Three 4" pieces of copper wire
- Six alligator clips
- 1.5V mini light bulb and holder
- Galvanized nail (nail covered in zinc)
- Penny or thick copper wire

Instructions: Use a knife to cut two slits in each lemon about 1/2" deep. Make sure that the inside of the lemon is exposed. If the skin is thick, make the insertion deeper until the fruit is exposed. Insert the copper wire or penny into one slit and the nail into the other slit for each lemon. Now, attach an alligator clip to each end of each piece of wire. Attach one end of the first wire to the nail in the first lemon. Attach the other end of this wire to the light bulb. Connect a second wire from the copper wire in the second lemon to the light bulb. Finally, using the third wire, connect the nail in the second lemon to the copper wire in the first.

Lemon Lessons

- 🍋 Your professional relationships are often some of the most enduring. They should be managed well to keep professional lemons from taking over your life.

- 🍋 Don't be afraid to negotiate for yourself so that you are not settling for less than you deserve.

- 🍋 Being a people pleaser at work will put you behind your peers. Be kind and assertive, you'll get further that way.

- 🍋 Pour as much effort into developing EQ as you do your IQ.

- 🍋 Learn to integrate cultural competency into your work environment until it becomes a way of life.

- 🍋 Respect is key!

Lemon Checkpoint:

- ⊘ What is the one major lemon you are experiencing at work? How is it impacting the other relationships in your life?

- ⊘ Have you lost your motivation at work? What can you do to jumpstart your drive?

- ⊘ How can you become more culturally aware in your day-to-day life?

When Life Gives You Lemons...Stop Making Lemonade

Chapter 5

Financial Lemons

Lemon Drop: *Lemons can be great for cleaning your cutting boards. Things like garlic, onion, and peppers can bleed into the wood, causing it to smell like a mishmash of dinners past. Odorous cutting boards can be the bane of any home cook or chef, and to avoid this you can use lemons. To find you how, turn to page 105.*

Regardless of who you are or where you've come from, I can guarantee that you have experienced a financial lemon...or several in your life. These lemons, if not properly dealt with, can become the root causes for the lemons discussed in the previous chapters. If you want to take ownership over your life and stop making lemonade, getting your finances in order is crucial.

Are You Financially Literate?

Being financially literate means that you are able to understand personal finance, money, and investments.

Most people are consumers but have no actual understanding of how their money works. If you don't understand how your money works, instead of making it work *for* you, it will work you instead. Have you ever heard people say, "I'm robbing Peter to pay Paul?" A person who manages their finances this way is not financially literate. In fact, they are potentially one disaster away from a major financial lemon. Though there are numerous components of financial literacy, we are going to focus on the top three: budgeting, managing debt, and saving.

Budgeting: Budgeting is not a luxury. You literally cannot afford not to have a solid budget. Some of you may be thinking to yourselves *I have a budget, but it doesn't seem to be doing me any good because my finances are still in shambles.* You are not alone. The majority of Americans have budgets that they don't stick to. One key that I have found helpful for sticking to a budget is treating it as a rule and not a suggestion. If you think of your budget as excessively elastic, it's easy to bend it to the point of uselessness.

An effective budget clearly separates needs from wants. This requires you to be honest with yourself. Your daily Starbucks coffee that you "can't live without" is not a necessity. If you can't give up your coffee because it gets you through the workday, start making it home to reduce expenditures. Budgeting isn't meant to keep you from enjoying your money. Its purpose is to help you enjoy your money on a continuous basis, not just that first week after payday.

Managing Debt: It can be hard to budget and save if you have crippling debt. For many, their debt comes from two places,

Financial Lemons

credit cards and student loans. Neither of these things are inherently bad, and there are benefits to both, they just need to be managed wisely. Too often, students take out an excessive amount of loans because schools are increasingly pushing loans as the primary way to finance a college education. Loans should never be the primary way to finance an education, and with due diligence, may not be necessary. One way to avoid excessive loans is to put in the work required to find scholarships and fellowships. Many schools have money earmarked for certain applicants that they don't widely advertise. Seek them out and apply, apply, apply!

If you do fall into the category of needing loans to subsidize your education, or your child's education, don't borrow more than what is necessary. Just because they offer you the maximum doesn't mean that you need to take the maximum. Take only what you need and pay attention to how and when the loans will incur interest. It's the interest that will cause the loans to take longer to pay back, not necessarily the principal itself. Also, many schools offer parent loans. Parents be careful about assuming responsibility for your child's education through loans, especially if you have student loans of your own to repay. You will be on the hook for those student loans, regardless if your child graduates or not. They also won't be obligated in any way to help you pay the loans you took out on their behalf because they are in your name.

Credit cards are another form of debt that entraps many. They can be great for building credit but are also effective at destroying credit. Try to keep your credit card balance to under 30% of your credit limit. If you choose to put your kids on your credit card to help build their credit, consider not giving them an actual credit card. It's so easy to think of credit cards as free money—don't. That's a dangerous slippery slope. If you are shackled by credit card debt, see if moving the debt to a lower interest-bearing card is a possibility, or seek out refinancing options to ensure that you are able to manage your payments. Whatever the source of your debt, make sure that your debt reduction plan is an adhered to part of your budget.

Saving: I used to pay myself last and then wonder why I didn't have a lot of money to show for my labor. I realized that the way I was approaching my finances was backwards. When you get paid, set aside at least ten to twenty percent for yourself. Doing this will force you to stick to your budget because you will be working with less than your total net income. It's sometimes good to budget as though you have less money available so that you learn how to live within your means.

You also need to have a savings plan for your emergency lemons. No one likes to be caught out there, but life happens. Don't wait until the lemons are spilling over into your life to develop a plan. Those who fail to plan, plan to fail. If you stay prepared, however, you don't have to rush around and get prepared.

An associate of mine, Maya, shared with me a story about how she had become homeless unexpectedly. She was in her early twenties and had moved across the country to start a new job. She hadn't fully prepared for this move and had next to nothing in savings. Things with the job did not go as planned, and her contract ended up being terminated early. Stuck 3,000 miles away from home, she began looking for other jobs and scrambling to find freelance work so that she could rent a hotel room and have food.

Eventually, she was able to get back on her feet and get situated, but she became materialistic. She was so traumatized from the experience of being homeless that she began accumulating stuff, forgetting that she was able to survive for months with one pair of shoes and three complete outfits. Maya, realizing that things won't protect her from poor financial decisions, has taken steps to get her credit back in order and begin saving so that she will never end up in that situation again. Life can come at you quickly; save now, your future self will thank you.

Do You Have Financial Boundaries?

We talk about boundaries in relationships often and boundaries are important. They can keep life's lemons from getting out of control. However, what is often not discussed are financial boundaries. Because we avoid talking about money, this is why finances break up more relationships than anything else. You have to be 100 percent clear what your financial priorities are and be willing to fight for them.

I once had a falling out with someone I had known for many years. I had quit my high-stress job and was just beginning to settle into my new career. Money wasn't scarce, but it was a little tight. I was just getting back to where I had been before my journey. This person I knew wanted me to go on a spur-of-the-moment trip along with a few other people. The trip was expensive, and I knew that with the financial goals I had in mind, it wasn't feasible that year. I told her that I wouldn't be able to go but was happy for the invitation. This acquaintance was pretty upset. She was a great person, but tended to be very overbearing at times, and I found myself often bending over backwards to please her.

She was so angry, that she refused to speak to me for an entire month. The old me would have tried apologizing profusely and finding some way to go. The new me, the one that understood that I had to have boundaries stood firm in the truth. I felt sad that our friendship could have been dissolved so easily, but I had begun to learn that being true to myself also meant understanding that I had to engage in self-care and monitoring all my needs, emotional, physical, and financial.

I didn't call or chase her down. The last conversation I had with her after that argument led me to tell her that while I appreciated her friendship, I also had goals and dreams that may not mesh with her plans all the time, and that was okay. I was sorry that she felt the way she did, but I wasn't going to jeopardize my finances for something that I felt didn't gel with my long-term goals. She hung up angry and I had to be okay with that. After a month, she called me crying. She told me that she valued my friendship and that she was sorry she had been angry. In fact, when looking at her own finances, she realized she shouldn't have been going either! She apologized and told me she respected my decision and she'd never do that again.

It took a bit of time for us to get back to where we were, and she had to get to know this newer version of myself, but I liked that she was able to come around and appreciate me. I learned an even bigger lesson from this: people treat you how you allow them to. How you allow them to treat you is often a reflection of how you feel about yourself. If you are being true to yourself and your needs, you wouldn't put up with disrespectful friends, friends or bosses. And people would be hesitant to do anything disrespectful because you've already outlined your boundaries.

Having financial boundaries will cost you, but the cost of not having them is even greater. It's easy when you are doing well, or are perceived as the one who is doing well, for you to become the community ATM. If you want to be the community financier, that's great, please disregard everything that I am about to say. If you are tired of being the community financier this is for you. You have to decide how much you are willing and able to give before lemons begin to appear. If you know that you are someone who is a natural giver, give yourself a charitable donation column in your budget. Don't be the type of giver though that gives the shirt off their back but then cries that it's cold. You need to take ownership of how you choose to spend your money. If you are tired of feeling as though you are hemorrhaging money, kindly, but firmly, tell those who think you have deep pockets, that the ATM is closed.

Don't Put All Your Lemons in One Basket

I made the frightening decision to leave my corporate job and go into business for myself. Being a freelancer is difficult and poses new challenges each day. One thing I've learned from experience, and those around me, is to never put all of your lemons in one basket. Even if you aren't a freelancer, you should never put all of your lemons in one basket. Career situations can change instantaneously, and if you aren't prepared, you can find yourself caught without a solid financial plan.

In order to avoid putting all of your lemons in one basket, it is recommended that you have multiple streams of income. There are several types of income, the most common being earned income, investment income, and passive income. If you are unsure of where to start with each type of income, network. Speak with those in your community who are where you want to be. Attend seminars and make the investment to create not just income but wealth that can change the trajectory of your family for future generations.

Lemon Solution #30: If your finances have reached a state where you feel they are beyond your capabilities, don't hesitate to seek out financial counseling to begin the process of restoring financial order.

Our finances can sometimes reek of past financial mistakes. Similarly, our cutting boards can smell like past creations. While you begin to clean up your finances, look at how to use your lemons to clean the kitchen.

Sweet Lemon Treat: *Cleaning Your Cutting Board*

Instructions:

The acids in lemons are great for cutting through odors. If you're washing your cutting board to no avail, try rubbing half a lemon on the board or try washing the board in undiluted lemon juice. You will have a cutting board that will be ready for your next culinary adventure.

Lemon Lessons:

- *⊘* Take ownership of your bad money habits and make a plan to improve your finances.
- *⊘* Don't be afraid to seek out financial counseling.
- *⊘* Budgets are not a suggestion.
- *⊘* Being charitable is great, but make sure you can afford it.
- *⊘* Plan ahead to avoid future disasters.

Lemon Checkpoint:

- Why do you feel it's so difficult for you to keep your finances in order?
- How do you plan to create additional streams of income?
- Create for yourself a 30-day budget that you feel you can adhere to.

_____

_____

_____

_____

_____

_____

_____

_____

_____

_____

_____

_____

_____

Conclusion

Celebrate the Small Victories

Before I had my child, I struggled with my weight. I would have an event and do a crazy fad diet. I would lose 20 pounds and then eventually find those pounds back...with a few extra. My weight lemons produced enough sour points to help produce massive amounts of lemonade. All I did was dilute what was going on with my weight and look for quick fixes. Once I went to an oral surgeon to have my jaw wired shut so I wouldn't eat. I lost 40 pounds over six weeks on a purely liquid diet. However, it was the same cycle. I would lose weight and gain more back. I didn't face the reasons for why I kept gaining the weight back, I just made more lemonade. People would tell me: "You have such a pretty face." "You hold your weight really well." "You dress nicely for a full-figured woman." The best comment I would receive was, "You have a great personality." These were all reasons that made it easy for me to be in denial.

Once I had my son, the weight piled on more than before. I began to emotionally eat, and I didn't feel great about myself. I got on a scale once and couldn't believe my eyes. I burst into tears. I didn't feel good at that weight. I had been denying my feelings about my body because I thought that I couldn't do anything about it. I was acting like a victim. I was acting as though someone was holding a weapon to my head and forcing me to consume high fat, high sugar over-processed foods. Ridiculous right? That's when I decided I had to be honest with myself and my feelings about food.

The relationship I had with food wasn't a healthy one. I went through periods of bingeing and near starvation. The pendulum swung so wildly that my body refused to lose anything. I felt lost. Then a dear friend said to me, "Do you want to be at your son's wedding 20 years from now out of breath and struggling because of all the weight you have gained, or do you want to be healthy, vibrant and involved?" That same friend reminded me that I was only seven years shy of the age when my father passed. It was a sour moment that caused me to really face the bitter. I had to make a change for the better and decide that I had had enough.

I had to look at what was fueling my weight lemons. Why was food a comfort. I read *Presto How I made 100 Pounds Disappear* by the magician Penn Jillette. His approach is bold, and he stresses ownership. Food is non-threatening. If you ate an entire box of honey buns people wouldn't judge you as much as they would if you smoked an entire pack of cigarettes. However, the side effects on your health over long term use are equally harmful. It's a challenge for most of us to hear the truth about our food choices and the direct correlation on our health and wellness. Another book that shifted my perspective and helped me conquer my weight lemons is *Eat to Live* by Dr. Joel Furhman. He introduces the Nutritarian way of eating where your main motive to eat is for nutritional wellness. I was eating as a means of socializing with my friends, and because it was centered around socializing, I viewed it as a benefit and not a deterrent. However, enough was enough, and I was ready to take supreme accountability. I enrolled in a gym and started working out with some accountability buddies. I installed a daily meal tracker on my phone. I decided to eat a nutrient-dense, plant-rich lifestyle for 90 days. I gave up sugary juices, coffee, and soda. I went to aerobic dance classes and started running.

It was not easy. I had to reprogram my mind and rebuild from years of bad habits. Instead of going to lunch and dinner with friends I would start suggesting active meetups like roller skating or swimming. I began to feel defeated a few months into my journey because I didn't always see the results. That's when my accountability buddies really helped. They kept me encouraged and motivated. I set a goal with some friends to run my 1st Half Marathon. I had even begun taking up yoga and I was able to achieve a flexibility that I had never had before. My friends and family were impressed, but, because I wasn't where I thought I should be, I didn't allow myself to celebrate the progress I was making.

One day, I looked in the mirror and had a long talk with myself. I decided that I would take it one day at a time. I took my scale and put it in a closet. I was going to shift my focus from losing weight to becoming fit. I focused on the feeling rather than the result. I loved feeling strong and able. There was something freeing about being able to race down a path and not be out of breath. I began to find the process as enjoyable as the feeling of having to buy a new pair of pants to fit my changing body.

We're bombarded by excess. Everything around us is often too much. We're overwhelmed by social media that tells us we have to be the next big thing, we have to have the best, most perfect lives ever. Everything we do has to be bigger, better and wilder than the next person. We have to have an over-the-top wedding, an over-the-top prom, and nothing that we do can be small-scale or little. We fool ourselves into thinking that the quiet, soft moments when we've achieved a small milestone means nothing. After all, how can you compare surviving a day outside the house with no triggers or flashbacks as a PTSD sufferer as a victory, when someone on your social media feed has just bought a shiny Lamborghini, is partying with a rock star, or just snagged a million-dollar deal?

Sometimes, it's the small, nearly unnoticeable things that we should celebrate. It's the things that we dismiss on a daily basis that create our realities the most. You may be battling a drug addiction and can say you've been clean for a whole year. You may have dreams of being a chef and just made your first dish. You may have started an exercise program and have pushed through it for a whole two or three months. Whatever your win is in your neck of the woods, notice it.

Look at the path you took to identify and deal with that lemon and recognize the bravery it took to get that moment. We are often so busy looking at the things we haven't done or didn't accomplish that we don't see the bigger picture. Big victories are important, but the small ones matter just as much.

I began to celebrate the small things. I cheered the fact that I could get through a hard-core kick-boxing class and have a good sweat. I honored the fact that my mind even began to feel clearer and my creativity seemed to kick into over-drive. I took each day as a time to be a better me physically. Along the way, I met awesome people that inspired me even more. I managed to lose eighty pounds. My body was even better than it had been before. I had become a happier and less stressed person. People noted my glowing skin and complimented how it seemed like I seemed brighter and more enthused. Then one day, I took out a pair of jeans that I had always tried to fit but never could and tried them on. They fit like a dream! I realized that I had crossed the finish line. Before I had crossed the finish line, I had had important experiences along the way. I had learned more about myself than I ever had.

Although I enjoyed being fit, I found that I had empowered myself. Recognizing the small wins was the first step towards getting the big victories. My weight loss journey had been one of my many lemons. I had to ask myself what I needed and wanted to do for my health and safety. I had to ask the hard questions and take a step in a different direction.

It takes a lemon tree nearly three to six years to begin producing fruit. I'm sure that along the journey the grower must learn patience, and must learn to celebrate the small wins, like the milestones the tree reaches, and the health of the tree as it grows. Once that tree has grown to maturity, it is worth the effort and the wait. Our lives often function the same way. The finish line is ahead of us, and it is attainable, but we have to learn patience and be willing to be happy with the small steps that lead us closer. Those small steps are what pulls us forward.

Be willing to give yourself a bit of credit for a small victory. You may not be at the finish line just yet, but you will be. Set small goals. Work each day towards something that you can reach and celebrate it! Even if it's as simple as getting an A

When Life Gives You Lemons...Stop Making Lemonade

on a test. Or being able to walk around the block. It could even be organizing that one closet. It could be anything that brings value to your life in a way that allows you to continue forward. Not only should you celebrate the win but reward yourself for doing a great job. The reward can be anything you desire as long as it doesn't push you away from your overall goal. Give yourself permission to buy a new book, get your nails done, or go to a movie. Remember, it takes a lot of patience to get to a goal or dream. You may have to take small steps instead of big leaps. And this is okay.

You won't be a success overnight, and Rome wasn't built in a day. You've got each day to make a small goal for a bigger dream. Take the time to recognize your efforts. Celebrate each win with friends, family, or a coworker. Understand that things take time, and, most importantly, don't beat yourself up if your overall goal takes longer than you expected. Instead, concentrate on what you've achieved so far. Lemonade was the quick fix, but you've opted for the journey. Enjoy the process!

Lemon Ledger

The Lemon Ledger contains all of the Lemon Solutions in a quick, easy to reference index format. For additional notetaking space, turn to the Noteworthy Lemons section on page 129.

Introspective Lemons (Chapter 2)

Lemon Solution #1: Evaluate the areas of your life where you often find yourself saying "yes," especially those circumstances where saying "yes" has not been in your best interest. Once identified, determine if those people, or things, are adding value to your life, or if they are an energy and resource drain.

Lemon Solution #2: If you feel that the chameleon analogy applies to you, write down those aspects of your personality that have remained hidden, along with why and for approximately how long. Then, see if adjusting towards reclaiming those areas of your life can be made in a way that doesn't change you from a people pleaser into a jerk.

Lemon Solution #3: Counseling is stigmatized within society because many take it as an implication that you are "crazy" or "unstable." However, to get to the root of self-victimization, help from a licensed professional may be appropriate and most effective. In the meantime, begin to make a timeline of your trauma, to see if the incidents intersect, or if they stem from distinctly different, roots.

Lemon Solution #4: Find out what you are afraid of that results in you procrastinating. Also understand that it is okay to be selfish with protecting your time. Block off your calendar or do what is necessary to ensure that you are not trying to fit more into each day than it can hold.

Lemon Solution #5: Eat Right – Stop eating on the run. Eating on the go exposes you to foods that are devoid of true nutritional value. Take some time to have a good, decent meal that's chock full of things you need like vitamins, minerals, and antioxidants. Eating right ensures that your body will be able to maintain your heart, lungs, and most importantly your brain (mind). Ensure you get the recommended daily amount of vegetables, fruits, and grains.

Lemon Solution #6: Drink Water – Hydrate yourself. We're 98% water and need H2O to power our skin, our hair, and our organs. Instead of settling for a soda, coffee, or juice, take things to a more basic level and drink water. If you want to drink water with a bang, try it with a bit of lemon.

Lemon Solution #7: Visit the Doctor – Regular check-ups are crucial to understanding the ways your body may be changing and growing. It's important to develop a relationship with a trusted medical professional and get regular screenings for your heart, eyes, lungs and any other potential issues. Cancer screenings are essential as we age, and for anyone who is sexually active, it's a must to have regular sexual wellness screenings. Make sure that you are doing all you can to be informed and stay in good health.

If you are a woman over the age of thirty-five don't feel embarrassed to get a mammogram. Breast cancer is a silent killer, and millions of women have been saved by just getting checked. Men should get checked for prostate cancer as part of their routine exams as they progress into their thirties as well.

Lemon Solution #8: Exercise – Thirty minutes a day is a great start! Take a walk around the block. Go for a jog. Get into the groove with a dance class or just dance around your house. Get out and get some fresh air and go biking on a trail. Take a friend or a close relative with you to keep you motivated. If you hate exercise, try something fun like Zumba or yoga. You can even do some low-impact water aerobics. Do what you like, but get your body moving so that you can get your heart pumping. Exercise helps to lower blood pressure and decrease stress. If you're a busy mom, a busy dad, or just plain busy, you probably can use a lot of that.

Lemon Solution #9: Decompress – Take time to read a book, watch a tv show you enjoy, or just watch videos of cute cats on YouTube. Whatever makes you relaxed, DO IT. Take a break and enjoy your day. Take a bubble bath or have a glass of wine. Do what it takes to get you feeling calm and serene. By decompressing, you are deactivating your flight or fight system. This will help reduce stress hormones like adrenaline and cortisol.

Lemon Solution #10: Talk to Someone – If you're going through a hard time like depression or experiencing suicidal ideations, it is imperative that you talk to a mental health professional. Even if you're feeling just a little stressed or out of sorts, having someone to help you talk through your issues can make you feel better about yourself and your situation. Don't think that your mental health should take a back seat. We live in a society that tells us "What doesn't kill you makes you stronger." But that's not always true. Sometimes it may not kill us or do noticeable damage, but life stressors can take their toll, nevertheless. There's nothing shameful about going to therapy or talking to someone if you feel as if your burden is too great. And if you need to unload on a trusted friend or family member who can give you the support you need, you should do that. Depression affects millions of Americans a year and can put you at risk for a variety of ailments, including heart attack and high blood pressure.

Lemon Solution #11: Take Up a Hobby – If you're the kind of person who puts everyone first and everything else on the backburner, it may be time for you to find something you like to do. Whether it's backpacking through the country, knitting, playing tennis or swimming, find something that is special and fun for you and just do it! Get out there and get your blood pumping with a hobby that is not only a great fun but is a great passion. Remember, a hobby is something that works for you.

If you've been secretly wanting to try your hand at something but are afraid of what others may think or of your skill level, well, there's nothing like seizing the moment! Don't live your life with regrets. Instead, think of an activity that would be invaluable to your mind and spirit and ignites your curiosity.

Lemon Solution #12: Say No – It's okay to just say no. If you don't have time for that PTA meeting, say so. If you would rather not participate in hosting Thanksgiving *yet again*, say so. We often feel as if we have to say yes to things that bring us stress in order to make others feel comfortable. Well, if you don't feel comfortable, there's no way you can really do that for others.

Lemon Solution #13: Get Some Sleep – We're bombarded by the message that sleep is for losers. In fact, one famous celebrity recently harangued an audience by stating that "You cannot sleep eight hours a day! Rich people don't sleep eight hours a day!" This is advice that is very crippling to men and women that already have round-the-clock duties. The truth is, we NEED sleep. It is one of our most basic biological functions. It is nearly as important as breathing. In fact, during an experiment years ago, soldiers were deprived of sleep for up to a week. After a few days, many of them began to have intense hallucinations and the experiment was forced to end. Another experiment had researchers waking people up right before they hit REM sleep. Many of them suffered ill physical effects, and this proved that not only do we need sleep, we need *quality* sleep.

After participants were allowed a full, uninterrupted night's sleep, they not only felt better but when they did sleep, they entered longer periods of **REM** sleep. **REM** (rapid eye movement) is often synonymous with dreaming. During this time, you can often see the eyes shifting back and forth beneath the eyelid. Therefore, the times that we dream are probably important for our brains. Neuroscientists don't know everything about our brains, but they do know that sleep and dreaming are important to our day-to-day health.

Sleep deprivation is associated with higher blood pressure, increased risk of diabetes, memory loss, and other health problems. So, don't listen to the mantra that you've got to grind 24/7. You can be successful in life and get a good night's sleep. In fact, evidence suggest that the way to be successful is to be happy, healthy, and focused. You can't do that if you're so tired you can't really think.

Relationship Lemons (Chapter 3)

Lemon Solution #14: Take a moment of self-reflection and make note of any harmful patterns that you see in the lives of your family members as well as in your own life. Ask the elders in your community, if they are available, where they think the root came from. Having done that, develop an action plan to counter these generational lemons. While doing this, also be sure to make note of the good fruit that you, or family members, have borne so that it can continue for future generations.

Lemon Solution #15: When your marriage is in trouble, it can negatively impact your ability to perform well in other areas of your life. If you see that your union is becoming undone, try seeking counseling if you're both open to it and committed to making things better. However, if you have both reached an impasse, be mature enough to understand that instead of laying blame, sometimes it's simply that you two don't mix well together, meaning that making lemonade would be impossible.

Lemon Solution #16: Understand that in relationships, sometimes things get beyond your control. You can't control everything; especially how other people perceive you. The version of you that someone else has created is not your job to manage. When you see that your "friends" are draining you, step away from the lemon juicer and move on; your time and emotional capital are much too valuable.

Lemon Solution #17: If you are dealing with a manipulative person, the best way to deal with this kind of behavior (if you have to at all) is to set firm boundaries and stick to them. Reframe their manipulative statements in a way that promotes your agency. The manipulator may try to further engage you in their machinations by guilting you for it. Don't fall for it. Stick to your guns, set clear boundaries, and understand that yes, they may be angry and disappointed, but they need to take ownership of those feelings — not you.

Lemon Solution #18: When encountering gaslighting, be it with family, friends, or co-workers, trust your gut and your instincts. If someone is trying to tell you something happened a certain way and you know for sure it didn't, don't accept their version of events. Stand firm. If you are repeatedly experiencing gaslighting, especially in work relationships, try documenting the situation. By having documentation it's no longer your word against theirs because you have evidence to add substance to your claims.

Lemon Solution #19: If you find yourself in a situation where money is being used as a means of control, there is a way out. There are tons of programs out there designed to help people to leave a controlling situation, and with today's expanding economy, it is easier than ever to make money on the side to save and then eventually leave. If you want to get out, you need to begin to set a plan in motion. For more details, see the chapter on financial lemons.

Lemon Solution #20: If you are experiencing abuse of any kind, call the National Abuse Hotline: 1-800-799-7233 or the Substance Abuse and Mental Health Hotline: 1-800-662-HELP (4357). If you are dealing with suicidal ideations, call the National Suicide Hotline at 1-800-273-8255.

Lemon Solution #21: Sickness and death are two bitter lemons that you don't always know what to do with. They come suddenly, and their bitterness lingers. There is no clear-cut solution, only that you need to give yourself space and time to process. Time may not heal all things, but it helps give you time to process. Focus on the memories and lessons you gained from their life. Allow those things to give you the propulsion you need to move forward but always remember their legacy.

Professional Lemons (Chapter 4)

Lemon Solution #22: Being passed over at work is a horrible feeling. If you see this is a recurring problem, begin to ask for 360 feedback, and conduct a S.W.O.T. analysis of your own performance. A S.W.O.T. analysis is a tool that measures Strengths, Weaknesses, Opportunities, and Threats. Though this is typically a business metric, don't be afraid to apply it to your own life to help chart your professional development.

Lemon Solution #23: The first step to successful negotiation is understand your industry or field. You want to be sure that the services you are providing are on par with the average. Research what leaders in the industry are doing and what others are pricing for their services. It may be tempting to "undercut" the competition, but you also don't want to cut your own bottom-line and profit margin. Become knowledgeable about the reasonable expectations of those working in your field, and don't settle for less!

Lemon Solution #24: To increase your self-awareness, keep a record of feedback received in order to see if there are any through lines. Also, pay attention to how people react to you, and how you react to others, especially in situations where you have felt triggered.

Lemon Solution #25: To improve your communication, try deep breathing to ensure that your response is tone appropriate. Also remember that emails can be tone deaf. If annoyed, take a few moments to gather yourself before responding to an email.

When possible also gather the input of others. If you still fear that you came across incorrectly, don't be afraid to follow up with a phone call or face-to-face meeting.

Lemon Solution #26: If you struggle with empathy, work on your active listening skills. Active listening includes listening to understand, not to respond. Active listening also means to not interrupt. Another way to increase your empathy is to not ignore the emotions of those around you. If you see someone is upset, don't put your blinders on; address it instead.

Lemon Solution #27: If you aren't motivated at work, consider ways for you to approach your work differently so that you can find enjoyment in it. Also try renewed goal setting. If this doesn't work, don't be afraid to find a new career that better aligns with your goals and current lifestyle.

Lemon Solution #28: Networking and social skills can be difficult for introverts. However, it can be worked through by finding a communication and networking style that best suits your reserved personality. Extroverts, take into consideration the introverts on your team. Too often introverts are expected to come out of their shells to meet the engagement of levels of extroverts. This can lead to burn out. Instead, sometimes it may be appropriate for extroverts to create a quieter, less energetically charged environment for a change of pace.

Lemon Solution #29: If you find that your diverse workplace isn't gelling the way it needs to, try attending the events held by the different diversity groups at your office. If your office doesn't have these, make it a point to get to know your co-workers. Ask (appropriate) questions and actively work to dispel stereotypes and biases.

Financial Lemons (Chapter 5)

Lemon Solution #30: If your finances have reached a state where you feel they are beyond your capabilities, don't hesitate to seek out financial counseling to begin the process of restoring financial order.

Noteworthy Lemons

Use this section to jot down additional notes on the lemons you've identified, conquered, or are undecided about. As you identify your lemons, don't forget to share them on social media using the hashtag #stopmakinglemonade.

_____

_____

_____

_____

_____

_____

_____

_____

_____

_____

_____

When Life Gives You Lemons...Stop Making Lemonade

When Life Gives You Lemons...Stop Making Lemonade

Noteworthy Lemons

When Life Gives You Lemons...Stop Making Lemonade

When Life Gives You Lemons...Stop Making Lemonade

Noteworthy Lemons

When Life Gives You Lemons...Stop Making Lemonade

When Life Gives You Lemons...Stop Making Lemonade

Noteworthy Lemons

When Life Gives You Lemons...Stop Making Lemonade

Bibliography

"5 Natural Homemade Astringents For Oily Skin." *NDTV Food*,
15 Nov. 2017, https://food.ndtv.com/beauty/5-natural-
homemade-astringents-for-oily-skin-1775822.

Beqiri, Gini. "The 5 Features of Emotional
Intelligence." *VirtualSpeech*, VirtualSpeech, 21 Sept. 2018,
https://virtualspeech.com/blog/5-features-emotional-
intelligence.

Brown Brene. *The Power of Vulnerability Teachings on
Authenticity, Connection, & Courage*. Sounds True, 2012.

Instructables. "Lemon Batteries: Lighting an LED With
Lemons." *Instructables*, Instructables, 4 Oct. 2017,
https://www.instructables.com/id/Lemon-Batteries-Lighting-an-
LED-with-Lemons/.

"Lemonade." *Wikipedia*, Wikimedia Foundation, 3 Oct. 2019,
https://en.wikipedia.org/wiki/Lemonade.

Norton, Ann, et al. "Thrifty Tip: Clean Your Wooden Cutting
Board with Lemon and Salt." *Happy Money Saver*, 12 July
2014, https://happymoneysaver.com/thrifty-tip-clean-wooden-
cutting-board-lemon-salt/.

"The 5 Components." Emotional Intelligence,
http://theimportanceofemotionalintelligence.weebly.com/t
he-5-components.html.

The Water in You: Water and the Human Body,
https://www.usgs.gov/special-topic/water-science-
school/science/water-you-water-and-human-body?qt-
science_center_objects=0#qt-science_center_objects.

"Types and Signs of Abuse." *DSHS,*
https://www.dshs.wa.gov/altsa/home-and-community-
services/types-and-signs-abuse.

About the Author

Leesa Askew is a transformational speaker and corporate coach who is passionate about supreme accountability, cultural competency and lemons. *When Life Gives You Lemons...Stop Making Lemonade* is a testament to her passions and how others can get rid of those pesky lemons in their lives. Leesa knows what truly drives positive transformations and results. It starts with self-assessment and taking supreme accountability with a healthy dose of motivation to succeed.

Leesa earned a Bachelor of Science in communications and journalism from the University of Florida. In addition to her professional and community initiatives, Leesa loves being a mother and wife. She currently resides in Jacksonville, FL.

www.ingramcontent.com/pod-product-compliance
Lightning Source LLC
Chambersburg PA
CBHW050123210326
41519CB00015BA/4084